TEACHING READING AND LITERATURE IN EARLY ELEMENTARY GRADES

Standards Consensus Series

National Council of Teachers of English
1111 W. Kenyon Road, Urbana, Illinois 61801-1096

Production Editor: Jamie Hutchinson

Manuscript Editor: Jennifer Wilson

Series Cover Design and Interior Design: Joellen Bryant

NCTE Stock Number 51930-3050

It is the policy of NCTE in its journals and other publications to provide a forum for the open discussion of ideas concerning the content and the teaching of English and the language arts. Publicity accorded to any particular point of view does not imply endorsement by the Executive Committee, the Board of Directors, or the membership at large, except in announcements of policy, where such endorsement is clearly specified.

Library of Congress Cataloging-in-Publication Data

Teaching reading and literature in early elementary grades.
     p. cm. — (Standards consensus series)
   Includes bibliographical references.
   ISBN 0-8141-5193-0
    1. Reading (Elementary)—United States. 2. Literature—Study and teaching (Elementary)—United States. 3. Education, Elementary—Activity programs—United States. I. National Council of Teachers of English. II. Series.
   LB1573.T389 1997
   372.41'2—dc21   96-54826
                                              CIP

CONTENTS

Introduction   *v*

1. Emphasis: Growth toward Reading

Zoophabets   *Dee Hopkins*   3
Changes, Changes   *Mary Dunton*   4
Owliver   *Lori Kochalka, Warren Smith,* and *Lora Langdon*   5
I Thought I Saw   *Mary Dunton*   6
Jack and Jill Were Risk Takers   *Jill Janes* and *Doloris Campbell*   7
Brown Bear, Brown Bear, What Do You See?   *Dianne F. Frasier*   9
Attending to Print   *Orysia Hull*   11
Reading for Fluency   *Ella Dawn Eiland*   15
Talking about Pictures   *John Warren Stewig*   16
Take-Home Tape Recorders   *Jane L. Decker*   18
Story Sequence   *Sue Winstead*   20
Comprehendos: A Comprehension Game   *Carole F. Stice*   23
Going for a Walk   *Jeannette Throne*   25
Team Learning   *Jane M. Hornburger*   27

2. Emphasis: Responding to Literature

Story Belts   *Jane Matanzo*   31
Mulberry Street   Joan Duea, Elizabeth Strub, Lynn Nielsen,
    and *Janet McClain*   31
Our Very Own Dragons   *Connie Weaver*   33
Examining Illustrations in Children's Literature
    Bonnie Ivener   35
Who Says?   *Joan I. Glazer*   40
Literature Groups: Intensive and Extensive Reading
    Ralph L. Peterson   41
Bridging the Generations: Helping Students Understand the Elderly
    Maria Valeri-Gold   44
Enriching Reading: Some Resources   *Alice Ganz*   47
Writing Haiku   *Adapted from an idea by Marlene Lazzara*   49

3. Emphasis: Integrating the Language Arts

Where Did the Bear Go?   *Lesia R. Lawson*   55

Learning from a Feely Box   *Ellen R. Smachetti*   56

Pooh Bear Visits   *Lynne C. Moore*   58

The Great Cookie Chase: Following Directions to Find
the Gingerbread Boy   *Beverly Simpson*   59

Bees, Bees, Bees   *Mary A. Evans*   60

What's Happening Here?   *Sandra Lee Smith* and *Willard Kniep*   63

Grow a Unit (From Turnips)   *John Warren Stewig*   67

Late Bloomers   *Pat Friedli, Nancy Dean,* and *Barb Burwell*   70

Troll Tales: Cumulative Literary Experiences   *Joy F. Moss*   71

4. Emphasis: Integrating Reading and Literature Across the Curriculum

Pasta Potpourri   *Robert C. Wortman* and *Jackie Wortman*   79

Robot Walk   *Shirley R. Crenshaw* with *Constance Guy*   81

Bubbles Throughout: A Week-Long Integrated Learning Experience
Wendy Hood   82

Learning and Writing about Magnets   *Sharron Cadieux*   85

Hatching Eggs and Ideas   *Mary R. Watson*   87

Writing as Scientists   *Judi La Due*   89

Competent Communicators   *Carol Hittleman*   90

All the Things We Can Do   *Brenda Parkes*   92

Read It with Music   *Debra Goodman*   95

I Can Read Nursery Rhymes   *Brenda Parkes*   99

Kaleidoscope Designs   *Nancy Riley*   101

A Classroom Time Machine   *Penny Rawson*   102

An Economics Lesson on Scarcity   *Willard Kniep* and
Sandra Lee Smith   104

Writing Postcards from Scratch   *Janis P. Hunter*   107

INTRODUCTION

RATIONALE FOR THE STANDARDS CONSENSUS SERIES

Much attention is given to matters that divide the teaching profession. But when NCTE collected dozens of standards statements, curriculum frameworks, and other key state curriculum documents in order to prepare *State of the States: A Report on English Language Arts Content Standards in Each State,* considerable agreement was evident in many areas of English language arts instruction. Similar consensus is demonstrated in the NCTE/IRA *Standards for the English Language Arts,* the core document that outlines national standards in our discipline.

A heartening fact has emerged from the standards movement, as varied as that movement has been: We are after all a community of teachers who draw upon shared instructional traditions in literature, composition, language, and related areas. Furthermore, in recent years the insight and invention of teachers and teacher educators have built upon those traditions in fascinating ways. The result is a rich body of practice-oriented material that parallels the mounting consensus in the profession.

NCTE has developed the Standards Consensus Series, then, in recognition of the existence of core beliefs about English language arts as revealed in innumerable standards-related documents and classroom ideas generated by teachers. The assumption underlying the series—and illustrated in it—is that good teachers have long been carrying out English language arts programs and classroom activities that exemplify sound implementation of the commonly held standards. The contents of each volume in the Standards Consensus Series were selected mainly from a database of classroom-practice materials. The database materials for elementary instruction were selected by teachers from a larger body of writings previously published by NCTE, mainly in the popular *Ideas and Insights* volume (Dorothy Watson, ed.) and in *LiveWire,* an NCTE periodical for and by elementary teachers and teacher educators that flourished in the mid-1980s.

In this volume we have gathered exciting activities that draw students in the early elementary grades into the wider worlds created in literature. The high value that our profession places on encounters with literature is plain from the sampling of state standards documents quoted here:

Alaska: Students who meet this standard will comprehend meaning from written text and oral and visual information by applying a variety of reading, listening, and viewing strategies. These include phonic, context, and vocabulary cues in reading, critical viewing, and active listening. (n.p.)

Colorado: Students read and recognize literature as an expression of human experience. (4)

Arkansas: Students will read to comprehend, respond to, evaluate, and appreciate works of literature . . . use prior knowledge to extend reading ability and comprehension. (4)

South Carolina: Students become familiar with the rich cultural heritage of language through experiences with literature. By reading and personally responding to a variety of genres, the learner develops into a lifelong and selective reader who enjoys a wide variety of literature. (15–16)

Alabama: Students will demonstrate knowledge of the types, periods, and characteristics of literature from diverse cultures and places. (n.p.)

Massachusetts: Students connect literature to personal experience and contemporary issues. (67)

New York: Students learn a wide variety of literary concepts commonly used in reporting on and discussing literature, including genre (poetry, novel, drama, biography, fable, myth, legend), plot, setting, character, point of view, theme, meter, rhyme scheme, tragedy, and comedy. (22)

Michigan: Students will explore and respond meaningfully to classic and contemporary literature and other texts from many cultures that have been recognized for their quality and/or literary merit. (25)

North Dakota: Students engage in the reading process . . . read a variety of materials . . . organize prior knowledge of a topic before reading . . . make and confirm/disconfirm complex predictions . . . generate questions while reading . . . use strategies for clarification. (12)

Similarly, the national NCTE/IRA *Standards for the English Language Arts* are rich in references to reading and literature. The standards call for reading a wide range of texts, classic and contemporary, from many cultures and for many purposes. They call for student understanding of literature in various genres and from many periods. They state that students must apply a wide range of strategies in order to comprehend, interpret, evaluate, and appreciate texts, noting the importance not only of learning to make predictions about and monitor what is read, but also of drawing on prior experience and engaging in interactions with other readers and writers. The NCTE/IRA standards clearly recognize the classroom as a rich site for strategy development, personal response, thoughtful analysis, and sheer enjoyment when students read—not only print texts, but nonprint texts as well.

The powerful statements of the importance of reading and literature expressed in the standards point to the usefulness of this collection as a key volume in the Standards Consensus Series. Of course, this is not to suggest that this book is of value only to those seeking to establish relationships between standards and instructional practice. Every elementary-level teacher of English language arts will find a wealth of lively, academically well-grounded ideas in this volume. Even if there had been no "standards movement" as such, these materials would nonetheless present a profile of exemplary practice worthy of emulation in improving students' enjoyment of and performance in reading and literature.

Surely, the early elementary years are key in setting the groundwork for students' literacy development. The child's eagerness to discover the universe of sights, sounds, colors, textures, and other wondrous signs and symbols can be turned toward the world of pictures and words found in books. There is adventure in attaching meanings to squiggles found on mysterious pages, and the early elementary teacher can build upon the students' linguistic strengths, opening the door to a road that leads to lifelong reading habits. The teaching and learning experiences in this volume demonstrate how teachers bring excitement to reading and literature instruction that is relevant to standards embraced throughout the country.

A few comments about the nature of the materials and their organization are in order. Consistent with NCTE position statements and with the texts of many standards documents, most of the classroom practices here do not isolate the teaching of reading literature from the entire range of English language arts skills and topics, or from the larger school curriculum. The materials in the Standards Consensus Series demonstrate amply that good teachers often do everything at once—asking students to reflect upon and talk about literary experiences, encouraging them to make notes about their readings and discussions in preparation for writing, and finding other ways to weave the language arts together in an integral learning experience.

A North Carolina goals document makes this point especially well: "Communication is an interactive process that brings together the communicator(s), the activity or task, and the situation that surrounds them. It is a constructive, dynamic process, not an isolated event or an assembly of a set of sub-skills. . . . Though listed separately, the [North Carolina] goals are not to be perceived as linear or isolated entities. The goals are interrelated aspects of the dynamic process of communication" (46). While the focus of this volume is mainly on teaching fiction, then, the classroom experiences typically exemplify the dynamics of real teaching.

ORGANIZATION OF THE BOOK

The materials in *Teaching Reading and Literature in Early Elementary Grades* are grouped in useful ways that will be described below. However, neither the arrangement of materials in this text nor the details of a particular classroom experience are intended to be prescriptive. The arrangement of the four sections is for convenience, not compartmentalization. There is no intention to isolate any particular aspect of literacy instruction from other aspects. Indeed, there is much fruitful overlapping of categories; for example, "Story Belts " and "Examining Illustrations in Children's Literature" are in the section that emphasizes responding to literature, but they include art activities that might also place them in the section that emphasizes integrating reading across the curriculum.

As for the details of the classroom activities, teachers who use this book well will invariably translate the ideas in terms of their own experience. Student populations differ; cookie-cutter activities simply don't work in every classroom environment. Most significantly, teachers know their own students, and they have sound intuitions about the kinds of ideas and materials that are and are not appropriate in their classrooms. From this solid collection of materials, teachers are invited to select, discard, amplify, adapt, and integrate ideas in light of the students they work with and know.

The first two sections of this volume focus on beginning to read and responding to that which is read. **Section 1—Emphasis: Growth toward Reading** acknowledges that reading is a holistic act rooted in abilities that evolve over a period of time. During this period the beginning reader learns to use prior knowledge about people, places, and things to construct meaning from texts. The ability to tap into prior knowledge will help beginning readers make logical predictions about stories before and during reading. Many materials in Section 1 are designed specifically to help beginning readers make predictions about a story or scenario that can lead to writing a story.

Motivation is another key factor in learning to read. The hands-on activities in items such as "Changes, Changes" and "Take-Home Tape Recorders" are highly motivating for young children. Another important characteristic of good readers is the ability to read fluently. Readers must be able to recognize and decode words skillfully so that the decoding process does not interfere with comprehension of the text. Activities such as "Attending to Print" and "Reading for Fluency" are designed to help students become smoother and more easeful readers.

The last four entries in this section focus on thinking abilities, beginning with a straightforward approach to sequencing pictures in logical order for a story. "Comprehendos" is more complex, calling for categorization of information from a text. The final item engages cooperative learning teams in a cognitively rich, enjoyable experience that elicits ideas that are both thoughtful and creative.

Section 2—Emphasis: Responding to Literature provides a wide variety of ways for teachers to elicit crisp student responses to literary works. Many items are also excellent resources; they provide lists of books, some familiar, some less known, for engaging students in the act of reading.

The first seven entries highlight enjoying and reacting to literature. They cover a wide range of difficulty levels, beginning with the simple paper constructions produced in "Story Belts" and going on to in-depth discussions in "Literature Groups" and an imaginative entry on developing empathy with the elderly.

The last two items in this section contain suggestions for the use of poetry in early elementary reading programs. An annotated resource list with related activities is followed by a well-articulated lesson on "Writing Haiku."

Section 3—Emphasis: Integrating the Language Arts includes activities that demonstrate multisensory approaches to instruction, often engaging students in the use of varied sensory experiences as well as speaking, listening, reading, and writing. Most of the ideas are also highly motivating: for example, solving the mystery elements in "Where Did the Bear Go?," "Learning From a Feely Box," and "The Great Cookie Chase" will be especially appealing to very young students.

The materials in this section are grouped roughly on the basis of increasing complexity. It begins with concrete tactile exercises and moves toward the cognitively challenging experiences in "Troll Tales: Cumulative Literary Experiences." Again, some items provide helpful lists of teachable works.

Section 4—Integrating Reading Across the Curriculum includes materials that emphasize connections between reading and other areas of the curriculum, namely math and science, fine arts, and social studies. The items are grouped by curriculum area, beginning with mathematics. The initial item, though, is appropriately called "Pasta Potpourri" in that it integrates many topics—cooking, math, science, fine arts, social studies, and (of course) language arts. Three math-oriented activities follow, then four lively activities that integrate the language arts and science are presented. The fine arts are next; but again, the initial entry stresses "*All* the Things We Can Do," from music to physical education to carpentry to cooking, and more. Finally, the materials on social studies demonstrate how compatible social studies can be with all of the English language arts.

The preparation of this volume revealed that many topics and concerns found in NCTE's previously published classroom practice materials on reading and literature closely parallel the foci of the state-level standards statements cited earlier in this introduction. In a time of considerable pessimism and discord in education, it is encouraging to find such grounds for consensus in the teaching of English and language arts. In the state and national standards, we find *common goals* for the teaching of our discipline. In the reported practices of the English language arts teaching community, we find *a formidable body of ideas about how to achieve those goals.* The Standards Consensus Series is both a recognition of cohesiveness and a tool for growth in the profession.

Finally, some acknowledgments are in order. First, kudos to the teachers and teacher educators who contributed their thoughtful practices to this collection, mostly via entries in NCTE's *Ideas and Insights* volume and past issues of *LiveWire.* The texts from those works are virtually unchanged, and the institutional affiliations of the teachers reflect their teaching assignments at the time of original publication. A few entries in this volume are from non-early elementary levels (i.e., from upper elementary teachers or from teacher educators who work with K–6 classroom teachers), but all were judged to be appropriate for use at the early elementary level by the teachers who reviewed materials from the database.

Issues of *LiveWire* and other publications which were sources for this text have been regularly reviewed by chairs of the NCTE Elementary Section and other NCTE leaders. The teachers who categorized the vast body of materials for inclusion in NCTE's general database of teaching practices are Kathleen Alexis, Alice Osborne, Kathleen Shea, and Susan Sheahan. This text was compiled by Alice Osborne, formerly a teacher at Villa Grove Elementary School, Illinois.

Introduction

REFERENCES

Alabama Department of Education. n.d. *Learning Goals and Performance Objectives.*

Alaska Department of Education. 1994. *Alaska Student Performance Standards.*

Arkansas Department of Education. 1993 Edition. *Arkansas English Language Arts Curriculum Framework.*

[Colorado] Standards and Assessment Council. December 1994. *Model Content Standards for Reading, Writing, Mathematics, Science, History, and Geography.* Final discussion draft.

Massachusetts Department of Education. March 1995. *English Language Arts Curriculum Content Chapter: Constructing and Conveying Meaning.* Draft.

Michigan State Board of Education. September 1994. *Core Curriculum Content Standards and Benchmarks for Academic Content Standards for English Language Arts.* Draft.

New York State Education Department. October 1994. *Curriculum, Instruction, and Assessment: Preliminary Draft Framework for English Language Arts.*

North Carolina Department of Public Instruction. 1992. *Competency-Based Curriculum. Teacher Handbook: Communication Skills, K–12.*

North Dakota Department of Public Instruction. 1996. *North Dakota English Language Arts Curriculum Frameworks: Standards and Benchmarks.*

South Carolina English Language Arts Curriculum Framework Writing Team. February 1995. *English Language Arts Framework.* Field review draft.

1 | EMPHASIS: GROWTH TOWARD READING

Books are springboards for many of the classroom ideas in Teaching Reading and Literature in Early Elementary Grades. *As the teachers often state, though, their ideas can often be used in connection with books other than the particular one cited or in connection with other motivators provided by an inventive teacher. The four activities below involve books that promote lively experiences with phonics, creative thinking and writing, and other literacy skills.*

| ZOOPHABETS

Robert Tallon's alphabet picture book, *Zoophabets* (Bobbs-Merrill, 1971), provides an excellent creative writing model for students to follow while, possibly unaware, they are reviewing letters and their sounds. The Zoophabets are imaginary creatures—one per letter of the alphabet—who live in places starting with the sounds of each letter and eat an appropriate diet of foods whose names also begin with that same sound. For example, the Indo lives in inkwells and eats inkblots, inkstains, and inkstands. The Obbey lives in orchestra pits and eats old opera stars, overtures, offkey organs, ovations, and oompah-pahs.

The language pattern and style of illustration lend themselves to replication, while the imaginative writing prevents the book from seeming condescending or too young for older students. The activity I use involves sharing of ideas and words as well as thinking about initial letter sounds. Here are the steps to follow:

1. Share the book with students by reading it aloud and displaying the pictures.
2. Let students warm up for writing by inventing a Zoophabet creature as a group. Help students think of both concrete and abstract words for where their creature lives and what it eats—e.g., a Pibble might live in a pillow and eat peppers, praise, and piano practice. Record students' suggestions on the board; then read them aloud and ask students to decide which sound best together.

3. Tell students that they will be creating their own Zoophabet creatures. Distribute sheets of black construction paper, 3" x 5" white index cards, felt-tip markers, and colored chalk.

4. Using a "draw from the hat" technique, ask each student to select a letter of the alphabet.

5. Encourage students to use their imaginations in inventing, drawing, and writing about their Zoophabet creatures. Students may have access to the dictionary and may seek help from their classmates if they have a hard time thinking of words to use in their verses. When all students are finished, ask them to read their Zoophabet verses aloud to the class in alphabetic order.

Dee Hopkins, Laramie, Wyoming

CHANGES, CHANGES

Changes, Changes by Pat Hutchins (Macmillan, 1971) is a delightful story in which colored wooden blocks are arranged and rearranged by the two characters to create whatever they need at the moment—a house, a fire truck, a boat, etc. Because this book has no words, it lends itself to use in oral storytelling and predicting outcomes.

As my students and I look at the book together, I encourage them to tell the story and to think about it by asking them what is happening and what they think is going to happen next. Then I give students colored blocks so that they can either build structures pictured in the book or create something of their own design. Depending on the students' abilities, I ask them to draw what they have created and then to describe it to me and their classmates, or I have them write a few words or phrases about what they have built with their blocks and then read their descriptions back to me.

For first and second graders, this activity could be expanded to include building and drawing a series of scenes similar to the ones in *Changes, Changes*, in which each situation leads into the next one. Students could then explain their story to their classmates or hold their pictures up and ask their classmates to talk about what is happening in each picture.

Mary Dunton, Glenn Duncan Elementary School, Reno, Nevada

| OWLIVER

O*wliver* by Robert Kraus (illustrated by Jose Arego and Ariane Dewey; Windmill Books, 1974) is a story about a young owl who tries to figure out what he wants to become when he grows up. His father wants him to become a doctor or lawyer, and his mother wants him to become an actor. But in the end, Owliver makes a choice of his own.

Owliver can be used with students from kindergarten up to third grade. Here are some suggestions for discussion and for writing assignments:

1. Point out to students that although Owliver likes to act and to pretend to be a doctor and a lawyer, when he grows up he becomes a fire fighter. Ask students why they think Owliver makes this choice. Pose questions that require students to respond to the story, such as:

    Why do you think Owliver likes to pretend to be an actor, a lawyer, and a doctor?
    Have you ever pretended to be any of these people?

    Then move on to questions that are less directly related to the text:

    What would you like to do when you grow up?
    Why have you made this choice?
    Do you think you might change your mind?
    What might make you change your mind?

2. Ask students if they think it is important for Owliver to become what he wants to become, instead of deciding to become a doctor, lawyer,

or actor, as his parents hope he will. Talk about what it means to make one's own choice.

3. Invite outside speakers to visit the class and to talk about how they came to have their current jobs or careers. Ask speakers to talk about why they decided to do what they are doing now, whether they tried more than one type of work before settling on their present occupations, and what they like about their jobs or careers.

4. Read the story a second time, and this time stop reading after the line "But when Owliver grew up, guess what he became." Ask students to think of a new ending for the story and to draw pictures that illustrate their own endings.

5. Ask your school or public librarian to help you find other storybooks in which the main character is trying to decide what to do when he or she grows up. Read several to the class and then ask students to talk about the different ways in which the characters make up their minds as to what they want to be.

Lori Kochalka, Warren Smith, and Lora Langdon, Mount Pleasant, Michigan

| I THOUGHT I SAW

I thought I saw a stallion gallop across the sky.
I pinched myself and looked again—
—A cloud was scurrying by.

The language pattern in *I Thought I Saw* by Pam Adams and Ceri Jones (Playspaces-International, 1974) is fun for children to read along with and imitate. The "I thought I saw" pattern is repeated on every two-page spread, accompanied by a cutout form that resembles the object described. When you turn to the next two-page spread, you see that the object is different from what you expected. This provides an opportunity to ask students to predict what they will see and read when the page is turned.

I used this book with second graders. I read each "I thought I saw" statement and then asked students to suggest all the possible objects they might find on the next page. After we read through the book twice, I handed students folded sheets of 12" x 18" white construction paper with which to make their own two-page "I thought I saw" episodes.

Another book you might want to share with your students as part of this activity is Tana Hoban's *Look Again* (Macmillan, 1971), which contains unusual photographs of textures of ordinary objects.

Mary Dunton, Glenn Duncan Elementary, Reno, Nevada

JACK AND JILL WERE RISK TAKERS

WHY

To help students become aware of the process of predicting, confirming, and constructing meaning as they read

WHO

Young readers who need to be encouraged to become risk takers

HOW

Use this procedure with the entire class so all children can become comfortable with predicting (taking a risk). Ask students to say various nursery rhymes aloud together. Pick out a favorite, such as "Jack and Jill," and print this on the chalkboard. As you point to the rhyme, say the beginning and let the children fill in the last word or phrase. Pick out other favorites and proceed in the same fashion.

Using the song "Old McDonald Had a Farm," pick out individual children to fill in the animal names. Continue until the children feel comfortable trying this. Then select or write a predictable passage involving a topic or characters that children are familiar with, such as the following:

> Tom and Jerry are my favorite cat and mouse. Often they get into terrible fights. One day Tom was asleep on his favorite rug. Suddenly a loud crash woke Tom up. He saw Jerry hanging by his _____. Tom chased Jerry around the _____. Tom soon tired out and went back to sleep on his _____. Soon Jerry was hanging by his _____. Because they are so funny, Tom and Jerry are my favorite _____ and _____.

Hand out written copies and ask the children to supply the missing words.

WHAT ELSE

Students might want to write their own stories with missing words, such as the one below:

> One spring morning I wanted to walk to school. I kissed my _____ goodbye. I opened the front _____ and walked outside. I looked up in the big tree and saw a little _____ singing. A dog _____ at me as I walked by. I saw some pretty _____ growing by the side of the road. Just then I felt a drop of rain hit my face. I didn't have my _____ with me so I got wet. I dropped my books and they got _____ too. I started to _____ fast. All at once it stopped _____ and the sun came out. Then I heard the bell ring, and it was time for school to begin. What a fun _____ I had.

Make copies for the other children and explain that they should predict any reasonable response for the blank spaces. Emphasize that many responses will be appropriate, not just one right answer.

After students fill in the blanks, display the text on an overhead projector and ask for volunteers to read their word choices aloud and to indicate how and why they chose these words. Encourage students to discuss the different meanings created by the different choices of words.

Jill Janes, Hannibal Public Schools, Missouri, and Doloris (Dee) Campbell, Columbia Public Schools, Missouri

BROWN BEAR, BROWN BEAR, WHAT DO YOU SEE?

PURPOSE

- To enjoy reading
- To gain skill and confidence in reading
- To create phrases and sentences that follow a simple language pattern

MATERIALS

- A Big Book copy of Bill Martin's *Brown Bear, Brown Bear, What Do You See?* (Holt, Rinehart and Winston, 1983)
- Paper, pencils, and drawing materials

Sharing a Big Book with a class recreates the bedtime story experience. Sitting comfortably in a circle, everyone can see the print and the illustrations and can share in the rhythm of the language. A Big Book can also serve as an excellent diagnostic tool when used with beginning readers.

I chose *Brown Bear, Brown Bear, What Do You See?* for its repetition, predictable language, and fine illustrations. (Many other Big Books lend themselves to the same treatment.) The students had gone to the zoo the day before, so the timing of this activity was just right. Before reading, I helped students focus on the story and draw on their personal knowledge. I asked them, "What do you know about bears?" One student replied, "Polar bears can camouflage with snow." Another said that he had seen "the American grizzly bear." A third answered, "Bears hibernate in the winter." *Camouflage* and *hibernate* are sophisticated words for kindergartners—examples of the wealth of knowledge that children may bring to school.

I showed the students the Big Book and began reading, encouraging students to read along. They read quietly at first, but as the language pattern became more and more familiar, their voices grew louder. When we came to the phrase "purple cat," I stopped to see if students could continue alone. One continued confidently, and later explained, "I can read 'purple' because that's on my word list."

Students were able to read the story without too much help. When they encountered the words *goldfish* and *teacher,* they were silent until they heard the words and saw the pictures. When we finished reading the story for the first time, I asked students if they would like to read the book again. There were smiles and nods.

Several student volunteers took turns pointing to the words on the page as the class read along. After the second reading, I asked such questions as "Who can find the word see on this page?" and "How many words are there on this page?" When we read the sentence "I saw a purple cat looking at me," I asked, "Can anyone find the two words in the sentence that sound alike?" A student immediately pointed to *cat* and *at.*

The students loved hearing *Brown Bear, Brown Bear, What Do You See?* a third time. This time they read even more confidently. I suggested, "Since we were just at the zoo, why don't we make our own stories? How would you start, Gretchen?" I asked. Gretchen replied, "Giraffe." I asked, "What color of giraffe? Can you say something about the giraffe that sounds like the story we've been reading?" Gretchen responded, "Black giraffe, black giraffe, what do you see?" A second student chanted, "I see a baby tiger looking at me. Baby tiger, baby tiger, what do you see?" Still a third said, "I see a green snake looking at me. Green snake, green snake, what do you see?" The students knew the language pattern of the book so well that they were able to enjoy creating their own story aloud.

Finally, students dictated their verses to me so that I could block-print them on sheets of paper. I handed these back to students, and they added illustrations to their verses. Not surprisingly, in more than one case the student's personal version of the story became his or her favorite reading material.

Dianne F. Frasier, Columbus, Ohio

ATTENDING TO PRINT

WHY

Current research into the reading process indicates that fluent readers use three cuing systems simultaneously: the semantic system or meaning of the language, the syntactic system or structure of the language, and the graphophonemic system or sound/symbol relationships of the language. The proficient reader samples from the print while relying heavily on the semantic and syntactic cuing systems. Occasionally, we encounter students who do not attend to print, often because they have had limited experience with books and thus are at the early stages of development in the reading process. The following teaching strategy is designed to give these students more experience in attending to print.

WHO

Elementary students who need additional help in attending to print

HOW

The following activity sequence develops a large cadre of familiar print materials. Each step builds on the previous one, increasing the amount of print processed but always blending this with meaning and the flow of language. Print awareness is increased through the production of student-made, teacher-made, and classroom materials. Throughout the sequence, provide daily opportunities for students to transact with print—both through the language of personal experience and through the more standard language of print.

Observation and Teacher-Child Interaction
As a preliminary step, observe the students in various settings to learn more about their interests and the important events in their lives. Then, in a one-to-one conference with the student who needs to attend to print, talk about these personal events or interests.

Bookmaking

Prepare an "I Can Read" Book for the student by folding four sheets of 8 1/2" x 11" paper in half and stapling them in book form. As the child watches, write the title "I Can Read" and the child's name on the book. Help the child select eight words for the book that are meaningful and significant to that child. Previous conversations or interactions will help identify appropriate words. Print one word at the top of each page, encouraging the child to read along and to predict what the word or next letter might be. Help the child use each word in a sentence and print the sentence underneath the word. The following is a sample of one girl's "I Can Read" Book:

Natasha
My name is Natasha.

Tyrsa
I play with Tyrsa at my babysitter's.

Aretta
Aretta always plays with us.

Ballet
Tyrsa, Aretta, and I go to ballet on Thursdays.

Mommy
My mommy is a teacher.

Daddy
My daddy plays squash.

King
King is our big noisy dog.

Baba
On Sunday we visit Baba [grandmother] Halayda, or Baba and Dido [grandfather] Powlowski.

Reading

When the "I Can Read" Book is completed, encourage the student to read the book often. Be available to listen to the reading and to help out if needed, or ask another student to assist.

Word Awareness

When the student feels confident about reading the book, ask questions about the print which help him or her focus on it. For example, the teacher working with Natasha might say, "Where is the word 'Natasha'? What other word starts with the same letter as 'Natasha'? Show me the word." Be aware of the child's word usage at other times as well. Some of the child's more meaningful words may be used in writing times— one indication of becoming more aware of print.

Experience Charts

Use the information in the "I Can Read" Book as a basis for a discussion with the child. Help the child expand the ideas, incorporating more of the child's background or experiences. Make an experience chart by printing the ideas, in sentence format and one sentence per line, on a sheet of chart paper. As you put these ideas into print on the chart, encourage the student to watch and to predict the message. The student confirms or rejects the predictions by utilizing prior knowledge, the context of the writing, and the letters and words being printed. The significance in this approach to teaching print awareness is that the meaning is paramount. At no point is print separated from meaning and relevance to the child's experiences.

Natasha's experience chart might look like this:

> My name is Natasha.
> I am four years old.
> Tyrsa and Aretta are my friends at my babysitter's.
> They are sisters.
> I play with Tyrsa.
> Aretta plays with us.
> Tyrsa, Aretta, and I go to ballet on Thursdays.
> We each have a black leotard and pink tights.
> We like to dance.
> My mommy is a teacher.
> She teaches nursery school and kindergarten.
> My daddy plays squash.
> He likes baseball, too.
> On Sundays we visit Baba Halayda or Baba and Dido
>   Powlowski.
> When we go out, King watches our house.
> He is our big noisy dog.

For approximately a week after making the experience chart, encourage the student to reread it and the "I Can Read" Book often. Be available to help the student with the reading if necessary. When the child is comfortable reading the chart, cut the sentences into strips and scramble them into a random order. Invite the student to sequence the strips in a logical order and to read the assembled strips.

Favorite Chant

Move away from personal experience texts to help the child gain control of familiar chants, poems, songs, even jump-rope rhymes. Select a chant that is a favorite of the student's and print it on chart paper. The student follows the same procedures as with the experience chart: reading the rhyme daily, finding significant words, locating words that look the same, and so forth. When the student has become familiar with the chant, cut the chant into strips and scramble the pieces. Ask the student to put the strips in the proper order.

In this activity it is important for the student to internalize the flow of language. Present the chant in various print forms so that the student has an opportunity to examine the chant printed in a book, handwritten on chart paper, typed on a sheet of paper, and, occasionally, printed or handwritten as a musical score. Encourage the child to write his or her own version of the chant. One first grader created this variation of Dennis Lee's "Alligator Pie":

> Alligator purse, alligator purse,
> If I don't get one,
> I think I'm gonna curse.
> Give away my teacher,
> Give away my nurse,
> But don't give away my alligator purse.

Favorite Story

The last step in gaining independence in attending to print involves the use of good literature. Select a predictable book of interest to the child. *Brown Bear, Brown Bear, What Do You See?* and *The Little Red Hen* are favorites.

First read the book aloud to the student. Then reread the book, encouraging the child to read along. Continue rereading the story until the child can read it independently. Repeat the procedures involved in the "I Can Read" Book, the experience chart, and the chant to foster print awareness. Next, ask the student to use the format of the predictable book to produce a personal book, recording one idea per page and including an appropriate illustration. The text of Natasha's book shows how she has reworked the pattern of the Brown Bear story:

> Natasha, Natasha, who do you see?
> I see Tyrsa looking at me.
> Tyrsa, Tyrsa, who do you see?
> I see Aretta looking at me.
> Aretta, Aretta, who do you see?
> I see Mommy looking at me.
> Mommy, Mommy, who do you see?
> I see children looking at me.

I see Natasha, Tyrsa, and Aretta looking at me.
That's who I see.

Orysia Hull, Child Care and Development Branch, Manitoba Education, Winnipeg, Canada

READING FOR FLUENCY

PURPOSE

- To practice reading aloud
- To develop reading fluency
- To feel more comfortable reading in front of a group
- To learn words from context

MATERIALS

- Copies of appropriate texts

By fostering confidence and interest in reading, this activity can help your students gain more from everything they read.

Choose a simple story to use in demonstrating fluent reading for the class. Before reading the story aloud, look it over carefully to note the pace, to look for rhythm changes, and to note the tone of voice and expression called for by the action and punctuation. After reading, talk with students about why you decided to read certain parts of the story with more expression and why you read certain parts more slowly or more quickly.

Next, select a nursery rhyme, a poem, or a short story and make a copy for each student. Point out the punctuation used in the text, and then ask students to "echo" you as you read. Read the text aloud, one sentence at a time, reading as smoothly as possible and with appropriate expression. After each sentence, pause and allow students to echo the sentence. Encourage students to try to read with the same pace and expression that you used, and not to hurry while reading.

Finally, ask for volunteers to choose paragraphs or short stories to read aloud for the class, and ask them to explain to the class which parts of the text they think should be read more quickly and which more slowly, which parts should be emphasized more, which should be spoken with more emotion, and so on.

You can also use a reading-aloud exercise to help students learn new words from context. Either you or a student volunteer first reads aloud a short text containing several words unfamiliar to students. Distribute copies of the text and ask students to underline or draw boxes around the words that they don't know. Students then take turns reading aloud sentences containing words that they don't know (with help from you if they need it), and talk about what each word seems to mean, judging from the context. Discussion and, optionally, a check of the dictionary definition will give students an understanding of the meanings of the new words. Then ask students to read the passage aloud as a group once or twice in order to grow more comfortable pronouncing the words they've learned.

Ella Dawn Eiland, Halstead Elementary School, Copperas Cove, Texas, with credit to Patti Matthews, DODD Schools, Panama

TALKING ABOUT PICTURES

About 80 percent of the information we process comes to us through our eyes. We are surrounded by pictures, yet we don't necessarily know how to look at, understand, or respond to them. One simple way to help students analyze what they see is to have them compare, contrast, and describe different picture versions of the same folktale. Many fairy tales are available in several versions, so check your school library for appropriate tales to select.

I start with two editions of *Peter and the Wolf,* one illustrated by Erna Voigt (Godine, 1980) and the other illustrated by Charles Mikolaycak (Viking Press, 1982). I read both books to the class and then reread them so students can take a second look at the pictures. Encourage students to talk about the characters, the scenery, the details, the action, and the colors. They might ask each other questions such as, What are the people's expressions like in this picture? How do they look different from the people in the other book? Does the background look the same? What colors are used the most in each book? Why? On the chalkboard we compile a list of similarities and differences that the students find in the two books, like these comments:

Peter and the Wolf, illustrated by Erna Voigt

■ Shows instruments on each page; other book doesn't
■ Pictures seem more like a story, done in cartoon style

Peter and the Wolf, illustrated by Charles Mikolaycak

■ Boy is lying on a stone wall; in other book he's standing behind a wooden fence
■ Grandfather looks meaner; boy looks braver, clothes are poorer

In addition to comments about the illustrations, students will probably identify similarities and differences in the language used in the stories. Later, you can focus on other paired tales in which the language is of more interest than the visuals, or follow up the group activity with individual conferences in which the student dictates comments to you. Following the initial group presentation, make the books available on the classroom writing table so children can study them at their leisure. Children can choose one of the two to discuss with each other or with you.

After seeing two versions of the Hans Christian Andersen tale *The Nightingale,* one illustrated by Nancy Burkert (Harper and Row, 1965) and the other illustrated by Fulvio Testa (Crowell, 1974), children dictated the following:

> *Burkert version:* I like the detail and the light colors. The pictures look real. The setting goes back and makes it look better. The people look Chinese. The real bird looks better than the artificial bird. The artificial bird is made of rubies and diamonds.

Testa version: I don't like the pictures because they look more like cartoon pictures than the other book. I don't like the pictures because they don't look very real. I do like the pictures of the fake bird because it looks like a chicken.

Using individual dictation with younger children gives them the freedom of fluency. You can encourage older children to write their own responses. Whether writing or dictating, students learn to use words to describe what they see and to make comparisons.

John Warren Stewig, University of Wisconsin–Milwaukee

TAKE-HOME TAPE RECORDERS

WHY

- To provide books and cassette tapes for children who are not consistently read to at home
- To provide children with good oral readers for models
- To provide children with the materials for assisted-reading activities at home
- To expose children to the sound of written language, which is different from the sound of the spoken language they are used to hearing in their home environments

WHO

Primary students, especially those considered remedial readers, and younger brothers and sisters at home; with adaptation, older students

HOW

After funds were raised by holding a schoolwide book fair, five tape recorders were purchased through a mail-order catalog. These were chosen because of their sturdy construction, simple operation, and safety features—they operate only on battery power. Sturdy bags with shoulder straps were donated to make it easier to carry the tape recorders, books, and cassette tapes.

When a student checks out a tape recorder for overnight use, he or she also chooses a book "package"—a sturdy, reclosable plastic bag containing a book, the accompanying cassette tape, and laminated directions for the use of the tape recorder (for parents). If the tape is recorded on both sides, a blank tape is included so that the child can record himself or herself reading the story if desired. A library card for each tape recorder and book package makes record keeping easy. Tape recorders and accompanying materials are checked out overnight or until the next school day. A penalty, loss of the next "turn," helps to get materials returned promptly.

While some commercial tapes are used, students prefer teacher-made tapes because of pacing. Look for thirty-minute tapes (fifteen minutes on each side) to save time and batteries winding and rewinding the unused length. When making your own tapes, tape on only one side, protect it by removing the appropriate tab, and let the children tape on the reverse side. (I have found it is better not to explain to the students how I protected the recorded side of the tape. I edit the directions that come with the tape recorder so that this information does not go home.)

WHAT ELSE

Older students enjoy making tapes for younger students.

Jane L. Decker, Columbia Public Schools, Missouri

| STORY SEQUENCE

PURPOSE
- To generate and focus ideas
- To arrange pictures in a sequence
- To construct a story from pictures

MATERIALS
- Copies of the handout

My young writers are enthusiastic about writing, but sometimes they become bogged down as their stories progress because they lose focus. A sequenced activity sheet (a page of four related pictures to be ordered and described—a sample appears on p. 22) helps students maintain their focus while they write, and also generates ideas for the story. These sequence sheets can be found in various supplemental classroom resources, or simple line drawings can be created by the teacher.

I give students a copy of an activity sheet, making sure that the pictures are general enough to allow many different student responses. I ask students to look at the pictures carefully. Pointing to each frame in turn, I pose such questions as the following to help students make sense of the pictures:

What do you see in this picture?
Is there any action taking place?
What might have just happened?
What might happen next?
How is this picture different from the one we just looked at?

As we talk about the pictures, I encourage students to think of the pictures as a series and to try to decide which of the pictures seems to come first, which second, and so on. I also prompt students to think about their decisions: "What particular detail in this picture makes you think it comes first (second, third)?" Examining the pictures and agreeing on the most logical sequence usually takes ten to fifteen minutes.

Then I ask the class to suggest all the words and phrases they can think of that relate to the pictures shown, or to suggest dialogue that might be spoken by the people in the pictures. I list students' suggestions on the chalkboard, creating a word bank for students to use later in constructing stories.

Next, students cut out each picture separately and paste the pictures in the order they desire on a separate strip of paper. I staple the sequenced pictures to the tops of sheets of lined paper. Students then create their own stories, inventing additional details about the people and actions shown and writing their stories on the lines beneath the picture strip.

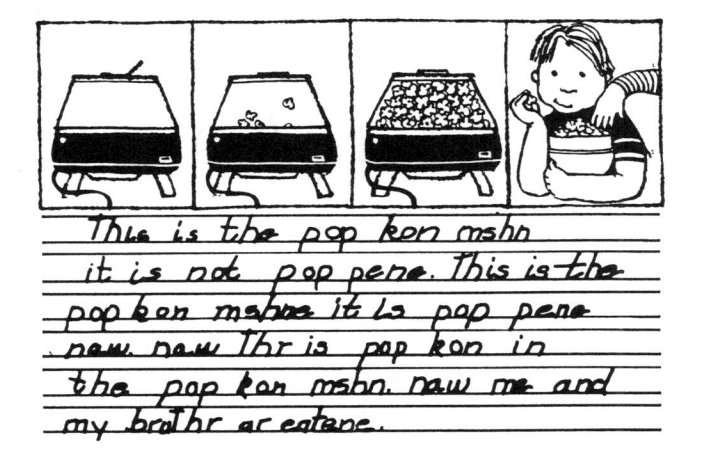

After a student shares his or her story with classmates, I place the story in the student's folder. The stories accumulate until there are enough to form a book. Then the pages are stapled together and the book of stories and pictures is shared with friends and family.

Sue Winstead, Hawthorne School, Bozeman, Montana

❧ ❧ ❧

Activity Sheet

COMPREHENDOS

A Comprehension Game

WHY

To provide students with an enjoyable way to begin analyzing and categorizing information available in a text

WHO

All elementary students who exhibit word-calling tendencies or who have difficulty organizing and remembering information

HOW

Prepare for the game by cutting thirty-five to fifty 6" x 12" cards from any stiff paper such as poster board. Draw a line down the center of each card with a dark colored marker, as if to make dominoes. Alternately print, on about 80 percent of the cards, one of the following words: Who, What, When, Where, Why, and How. Put two words on several cards. Leave the remaining cards completely blank. When you are satisfied that there are enough cards and options for two to four players, laminate the cards or cover them with adhesive-backed paper.

Ask students to read a narrative story or expository text. Discuss the reading with them, extending and elaborating their background of knowledge, the visual images, their vocabularies, and so on.

Provide students with felt-tip markers or grease pencils that will erase from laminated surfaces with a tissue. Shuffle the cards and deal them face down, dividing them evenly among the players.

As in dominoes, the first play is a double card containing two words. The first player writes on the blank half of one of his or her cards an answer from the story or text selection that answers the question posed by one of the two original words, such as "Grandma's house" in response to Where. This card is positioned next to the original card. The game proceeds with players matching their cards with those already played, supplying the necessary information where blanks occur.

The children moderate the answers. Challenges can be referred to the text, the teacher, or another child who is familiar with the material but who is not playing the game.

The floor might work best for the game since the cards are spread over a large area as the game proceeds. Displays of the complete Comprehendos game design make interesting reading for the other students before the pieces are dismantled.

I do not include a scoring system or points system, since I encourage children to play for fun and to help each other, rather than play competitively. However, if the children prefer competitive games, a point system can easily be worked out.

WHAT ELSE

1. Students may wish to draw pictures on the cards rather than write their answers. A combination of words and pictures can also be quite interesting.
2. Semantic mapping and story wheels are a logical extension of this experience. Children who have played Comprehendos seem to catch on to mapping strategies quickly.
3. Rewriting the material into a newspaper article or a news release is a logical follow-up since the cards call for answers to the five W questions.
4. A cartoon strip rendering of the story can work well following a game of Comprehendos. After students have broken down the story into its various elements, it's a good idea for them to return to the whole story.

Carole F. Stice, Tennessee State University, Nashville

GOING FOR A WALK

PURPOSE

- To read and compare books in which the main characters go on special walks
- To talk in small groups about the possible purposes for going on a walk
- To listen to and act out poems about movement
- To practice observing while walking

MATERIALS

- Assorted books which feature the main character going on a special walk
- Several poems about movement

While nature walks have long been part of the primary science curriculum, you may find it worthwhile to develop the theme of "Going for a Walk" into its own language unit. These activities can be adapted for use either before or after a class walk.

Read aloud to your students a book in which the main character goes on a special walk. Some possibilities are *Rosie's Walk* by Pat Hutchins (Macmillan, 1968), *Just Me* by Marie Hall Ets (Viking Press, 1965), *Spot's First Walk* by Eric Hill (Putnam, 1981), and *Four Fur Feet* by Margaret Wise Brown (Young Scott Books, 1961). Ask students, "What happens on these walks?" "Where are the characters going?" "Do they discover anything special?" "What special things might we (or did we) discover on our walk?" Students can prepare maps or murals showing the route taken and the sequence of events in one or more of the books. After the class walk, they can prepare a map showing the route and sequence of events in their own walk.

Another option is to let students pair up or form small groups and talk about walking. Ask students the following questions:

When can we walk to our destination, and when do we have to use other means of transportation?

Do you like to walk? Why or why not? How far do you think you walk every day?

What do you do or think about while you walk? What do you see, hear, smell, and imagine while you walk?

Do you know any people who walk for their health? In what ways is walking good for people?

To incorporate the arts, dramatize the different ways animals walk and move. Read aloud and act out the poem "Jump or Jiggle" by Evelyn Beyer (in *Time for Poetry,* compiled by May Hill Arbuthnot and Shelton L. Root, Jr., Scott Foresman, 1968); then help students think of ways that various animals move. Let students act out the movements of different animals to the beat of a drum. For example, you can ask students one at a time or in pairs to gambol like lambs, stalk like lions, or scamper like squirrels. Follow up this activity with the poem "About Feet" by Margaret Hillert (in *The Random House Book of Poetry for Children,* edited by Jack Prelutsky; Random House, 1983). Ask students, "How many feet do spiders have?" "How many feet do centipedes have?" (Spiders have eight, and centipedes, despite popular misconceptions, can have from 15 to over 180 pairs of legs.) Then discuss the many ways that people can move with their feet. List verbs on the board—*hop, march, skip, run, jump, leap, parade,* and others. After making a long list, you can ask for a volunteer to choose one of the words on the list and, without telling the rest of the class what it is, to move across the room demonstrating that word. The rest of the class can guess which word the student picked, and then another student may demonstrate a different verb.

Think of reasons to go on walks around your school, encouraging students to observe their surroundings carefully. We went for a "green walk" in September to see what was green. We went on a "changes walk" in October. Students noticed that the oak and maple leaves and the acorns had changed color, but the grass and evergreens were still green. At another time we may go on a "funny shape" walk where we look for funny shapes, or on a walk where we look for things that move or don't move. Or we may go on a "space walk" and pretend there is no gravity. Students have also suggested "flower walks" and "bug walks." What kind of walk will you and your students take? Let your imaginations roam.

Jeanette Throne, Shaker Heights School District, Shaker Heights, Ohio

| TEAM LEARNING

WHY

Team learning is an effective method for developing and strengthening language arts abilities. Experience shows that the more opportunities students have to discuss their ideas and to listen to those expressed by peers, to plan together, and to work out solutions to problems, the more proficient they become in all areas of the language arts. One of the greatest benefits of team learning is its versatility. It can be used to work out solutions to classroom problems, to study current events, and to conduct studies in content areas.

Team learning removes the risk-taking factor that discourages some children from participating fully in whole class activities. It is a vehicle for productive group interaction and allows less able students to benefit from sharing an assignment with more able peers. Completing a team task usually requires diverse talents and contributions; this cooperative effort enables every member of the group to contribute ideas.

WHO

All elementary students

HOW

Children's literature, by its very nature, reflects various predicaments, problems, and alternative solutions that stimulate personal reactions. It covers a wide range of subject areas and is rich with human experience, thus supplying a wellspring of situations for team learning.

After a book has been read to or by the children, divide the class into teams of three to six students. Give each team a page containing an assignment. Team members select a recorder and then discuss the task to be completed, as the recorder makes note of the group's decision or solution. Teams choose a creative way in which to share their findings with the other students, such as a panel discussion, a debate, an interview, or role playing. Students listen, ask questions when necessary, and participate in a discussion of each team's findings.

During the reading of "The Emperor's New Clothes" by Hans Christian Andersen, several students in one class expressed opinions about some of the characters and incidents in the story. During the team learning, they had an opportunity to discuss the story in depth, reacting to story situations and raising questions not fully covered in the brief class discussion. Students discussed the following questions, decided on their responses, and presented the information to their classmates:

1. Discuss some thoughts that the swindlers might have had as they explained the "fine stuffs" to the Emperor and worked late at night on the "magic cloth."
2. Do any thoughts (or words) of the minister indicate that he might have been afraid of becoming discredited? Explain.
3. What might the townspeople have said about the Emperor after the procession?
4. Why did the Emperor continue the procession after the people announced that he had no clothes on?
5. What reasons might the officials have had for pretending to see colors and designs in the cloth?
6. Why has this story lasted for centuries? Does this kind of thing happen today?

Jane M. Hornburger, Brooklyn College, City University of New York

2 | EMPHASIS: RESPONDING TO LITERATURE

STORY BELTS

After your kindergartners have heard or read a number of stories, story belts give them a chance to choose their favorites and to tell the world about them. Prepare the belts by cutting 25" x 4" strips of tagboard. Punch two holes at each end and fasten strands of yarn through the holes to be used as ties.

After choosing a favorite story, each student can copy a favorite line from the story onto the belt and draw pictures in the remaining space on the belt to show what is happening in that scene. Help students tie on their belts and give them plenty of time to circulate around the room to read each other's belts. Later in the year you might try a variation, such as creating "riddle belts" on which students write questions about a story read in class to be answered by their classmates, or "character belts," each one displaying a picture of a character from a book and a quotation from that character.

Jane Matanzo, Westminster, Maryland

MULBERRY STREET

If two words can capture the spirit of the typical first grader, they are *energy* and *imagination*. Students are bound to lose some of their excess energy over time, but if they learn while young to value and express their creativity, they need never stop imagining.

Books by Theodore Geisel, who is better known as Dr. Seuss, help young students to recognize and appreciate imaginative language and art. Geisel is sensitive in his writing to the rhythm and sounds of our language, and both story lines and illustrations are wonderfully inventive. A reading and discussion session on *And to Think That I Saw It on Mulberry Street* (Random House, 1989) is readily expanded to include the expression of students' own fanciful ideas in words and in drawings.

And to Think That I Saw It on Mulberry Street is the story of a boy whose imagination conjures up an amazing parade of objects, characters, and happenings. First, read the story aloud, allowing students to examine the illustrations as you read. Ask them to identify the events that are "really taking place" on Mulberry Street and those events that the boy's imagination is creating. (This could be done during a second reading.) Is Mulberry Street real? Are there any human characters in the story that are *not* thought up by the boy's imagination? Are there any animal characters that are not part of his imagination?

Encourage students to pay close attention to the illustrations as the story progresses. They can point to the parts of the illustration that they believe to be imagined (not really happening on Mulberry Street). How do the scenes change as the story progresses? What is added in each scene?

To prepare students to put their own imaginings into words, ask them to describe what they saw on their way to school. Using one of their responses, such as "a VW," encourage students to take turns expanding on this description, adding one element at a time, as was done in the story. "I saw a VW with zebra stripes." "I saw a VW with zebra stripes and no wheels." "I saw a VW with zebra stripes and no wheels being pulled by four huge mammoths." "I saw a VW with zebra stripes and no wheels being pulled by four huge mammoths on roller skates."

As students continue on this spree of imagination, distribute sheets of drawing paper and ask them to draw their ideas while they talk, as well as to write captions if they want. Point out that when students draw their thoughts, they are doing the same thing that Dr. Seuss does when he illustrates his books. The completed drawings can be taped to one wall of the room in a continuous strip (to show the sequence), ensuring that students have a chance to appreciate and feel proud of what their imaginations can do.

Joan Duea, Elizabeth Strub, Lynn Nielsen, and Janet McClain, Price Laboratory School, Cedar Falls, Iowa

OUR VERY OWN DRAGONS

Would you like a dragon for a pet?" When you ask this question of first graders, you are likely to hear a lively debate covering the pros and cons of dragon ownership. This question and others introduce students to an activity integrating reading, discussing, writing, and art, an activity that gives them a chance to create their very own dragons.

Students' imaginations are stimulated when they read books about dragons. As they plan and construct their own Play-Doh dragons, they find it natural to talk and write about what they are doing. By writing as well as they can without worrying about spelling, sentence structure, or handwriting, they take full advantage of what they know about language. As an added benefit, a group reading session helps students to discover that they are capable of reading their own writings to their classmates.

Begin introducing the activity by asking students such questions as the following:

Do any of you have pets?
Would you like a dragon as a pet?
What special powers do dragons have?
If you had a dragon, what would you and the dragon do for fun?

After students share some of their own ideas about dragons, pass around several storybooks that feature dragons. A book such as Tomi de Paola's *The Knight and the Dragon* (Putnam, 1980) may be best used in a small group, where students can work through the simple text at their own pace and talk about the meaning of each picture. Students may want to examine other books such as Jack Kent's *There's No Such Thing as a Dragon* (Golden Press, 1975) and Ned Delaney's *One Dragon to Another* (Houghton Mifflin, 1979) and then hear these books read aloud.

Spend a little time discussing the books, asking students how dragons are presented in each book, and finding out what they liked best in each. Then ask students to create their own dragons. Student volunteers can help you pass out portions of Play-Doh or homemade clay (the recipe can be found in most primary craft guides), pipe cleaners, pasta twists, split green peas, and dried beans.

As students shape and decorate their dragons, the comments they make among themselves are likely to be about the things that their dragons can do and about the various body features that they are giving their dragons. Encourage them to talk too about how their dragons will be similar to or different from the dragons in the books.

When students finish constructing their dragons, give them a chance to put down in writing some of the ideas that they discussed as they worked. Whether students want to write stories, paragraphs, or captions for drawings, make sure that they don't worry too much about spelling or neatness. Have crayons and markers on hand so that students can illustrate their papers, and encourage them to share their work with classmates sitting nearby. Then when students have recorded all that they want to say about their dragons, they can gather together on a reading rug (or the equivalent) and take turns reading their stories aloud and showing their drawings. Students should be able to read almost all of what they've written (though some may stumble a bit at first), and they obviously enjoy the chance to communicate with an appreciative audience.

If you can obtain the use of a camera that provides instant prints, preserve the moment by taking a picture of each student with his or her clay dragon. The clay dragons can be displayed on a table at the side of the room, and the photographs, as well as the students' writings and drawings, can be posted on the classroom bulletin board under the label "Our Very Own Dragons."

Connie Weaver, Western Michigan University, Kalamazoo, Michigan

EXAMINING ILLUSTRATIONS

In Children's Literature

WHY

- To develop students' understanding of picture book illustrations and their relationship to the story
- To foster students' strategies of observing, comparing, classifying, hypothesizing, organizing, summarizing, applying information, and criticizing
- To familiarize children with the methods and materials used by picture book illustrators through art experiences with various media
- To integrate children's personal experiences into themes of picture books
- To expand students' understanding of book binding and photocopying
- To develop students' awareness of characterization

WHO

Students in grades 1–3

HOW

For the activities that follow, collect a variety of picture books for children to examine, including such authors and illustrators as Ezra Jack Keats, Mitsumasa Anno, Jose Aruego, Marcia Brown, Raymond Briggs, John S. Goodall, Susan Bonners, Ed Young, Peter Spier, Leo Lionni, Gerald McDermott, and Wesley Dennis.

The following sample questions and procedures might be used in the three-week sequence of activities listed below as students examine illustrations in children's literature:

1. Observing
   a. What do you see in this picture that looks real or alive?

      b.   What do you see in this picture that was made with paint?

      c.   What do you notice in this picture that was not made with paint?

      d.   What do you see happening?

2. Comparing

      a.   How does this picture resemble that picture?

      b.   How is this book like or different from that book?

      c.   What changes have taken place in this story, considering the pictures only?

3. Classifying

      a.   Would this picture book become one of your favorites? Why or why not?

      b.   Is the mood of this story happy or sad? sad and lonely? sad and then happy? sad throughout? happy throughout?

      c.   Which colors seem to express the sad parts of the story?

      d.   Which colors seem to express a happier theme?

4. Hypothesizing

      a.   What do you suppose this story will be about? Why?

      b.   What kind of media did the illustrator use? Why do you think that?

      c.   What kind of person do you think this character will be? Why?

5. Organizing

      a.   Tell in sequence what the artist did to create this story.

      b.   Illustrate an important part of the story using any media available.

6. Summarizing

      a.   Dictate a summary of the story.

      b.   Illustrate the theme of this story.

7. Applying

      a.   Use a collage technique to illustrate something you experienced.

      b.   Make a collage for one of these themes: a rainy day, playing with friends, a family event, being with animals, the scariest thing, the funniest thing, being lonely, getting hurt, growing, losing something, taking a trip.

8. Criticizing

      a.   What do you like or dislike about the artwork in this book? Why do you feel that way?

      b.   Do you think the illustrations do a good job of telling or helping to tell what the story is about? Why?

      c.   What do you think would have been a better technique for the artist to use in illustrating the characters in this story? Why do you think that?

Week One

Share the illustrations from a variety of picture books. Have children tell what materials and techniques they think were used by the illustrators. Then provide materials for painting. The children might want to experiment with tissue paper and water as a medium to create a wash effect on paper. Invite the children to write a story to accompany their paintings. Read aloud *The Snowy Day* by Ezra Jack Keats and discuss the artistic techniques.

Prepare a chart on the chalkboard for listing children's ideas regarding "How a Picture Book Is Made." Have children express their ideas about what tools and materials might be used, what procedures are undertaken by someone who wants to publish a book, and how ideas for stories and illustrations are decided upon. Present the filmstrip and accompanying tape by Weston Wood titled *How a Picture Book Is Made: The Island of the Skog,* which features the book by Steven Kellogg. Then have the children talk about which of their ideas were discussed in the filmstrip and tape. Keep the list posted for future reference and add ideas to it as children's knowledge grows.

Set up a book-binding work area, including such materials as different sizes and types of paper, magazines, wallpaper books, a stapler, yarn, metal rings, and chicken marking bands. Display resource and reference texts about book binding and the publishing industry. Children may bind blank books or may prepare books for specific writing projects. The work area becomes the place to go when other work is completed. If available, bring a spiral book-binding machine into class. After children are familiar with using it, they may want to write about how the machine works.

Share the illustrations in *Louie, Peter's Chair, A Letter to Amy, Goggles,* and *Hi, Cat!,* all by Ezra Jack Keats. Have the children brainstorm a list of traits displayed by the characters and encourage them to share personal experiences that involve these traits.

Week Two

Set up a collage work area where children can mix paints, cut out designs found in fabrics, magazines, and wallpaper books, and glue materials to paper to express in pictorial form something they like to do. Invite them to write an accompanying story. Display the collages and ask students to read aloud their stories as the others in the class try to match the text to the picture.

Arrange to use the photocopier in your school. Bring children to the machine in small groups with their collages. Tape-record their comments as they predict what will happen when their illustrations are copied. Later, transcribe the taped comments and display them with the collages and the photocopies.

Read to children Tana Hoban's *Is It Red? Is It Yellow? Is It Blue?* Have children feel objects and materials in the room, and list their comments. Riddle form works well: "It's rough and has a point. It's a _____." Have children write their own books of sensory riddles. Older children may try their hand at writing sensory riddles about objects portrayed in such picture books as *Over in the Meadow* and *The Snowy Day* by Ezra Jack Keats, *Inch by Inch* and *Alexander and the Wind-Up Mouse* by Leo Lionni, *Anansi the Spider* by Gerald McDermott, and *The Very Hungry Caterpillar* by Eric Carle.

Share records and filmstrips of books like *Apt. 3, The Snowy Day,* and *John Henry: An American Legend* (all by Keats) and discuss the effect (or lack of effect) of the music on the story. Have children make instruments, or use available ones in your school, to accompany your reading of *The Winter Picnic* by Robert Welber, *We Came a-Marching . . . 1, 2, 3* by Mildred Hobzek, *Freight Train* by Donald Crews, and a version of *The Farmer in the Dell.* Tape-record each child's reading of a picture book, accompanied by an instrument or sound effects.

Visit the neighborhood library. In preparation, have children write a list of questions to ask regarding illustrators, types of illustrative techniques, standards for judging a picture book, and available resources for reviewing picture books. En route to and from the library, have children make chalk or crayon rubbings of objects they pass. Then cut the rubbings into shapes and invite children to glue the shapes into blank bound books in which they write about their trip to the library.

Week Three

Incorporate picture books into lessons and activities involving a theme or concept your class is studying, such as plants, eggs, sand, weather, or space. Display the books and have children vote for their favorite illustrators. Then bring in other books by the same illustrators and discuss with children the similarities and differences in technique, color, and overall format.

Set up a table containing paper, a pan of water, and two or three colors of enamel oil paint. Have children dribble oil paint into the water, swirl it gently, and lay a sheet of paper on top of the design. Carefully remove the paper by lifting a corner and dry the paper overnight. Then have children write the directions for making their unique designs.

Invite children to make hand silhouettes by placing their hands in front of the light of a projector and to make up a dramatization involving their silhouettes. Then have children cut out a person, some furniture, and a favorite object from black paper. Ask them to write about what the person will do with the object, who the person might be, and where the story is taking place. The cutouts are then arranged and pasted to the marbleized paper described above. (The reverse of this artwork can be produced by having the children make their cutouts out of the marbleized paper and glue these to black paper.)

Examine Leo Lionni's *Swimmy* with the children. Demonstrate how patterns can be repeated in illustrations by dipping such materials as doilies and rubber stamps in ink or watercolors. Let children try the technique and look for pages in *Swimmy* that may have been created in this manner.

Invite the children to make accordion-style books, illustrating each page with an animal that they know something about. Next ask the children to write a factual piece concerning their animals. Have them share their writings with other students and request editing suggestions. On the final page, the children write a poem or story involving the animal.

WHAT ELSE

Assemble *Louie, Peter's Chair, A Letter to Amy, Goggles* and *Hi, Cat!,* all by Ezra Jack Keats. Prepare five charts divided into thirds with these discussion headings:

1. What is the main character like?
2. What are three important things he or she seems to be doing?
3. Would you like this character to be your friend? Why or why not?

Divide the class into five groups and request that each group choose a scribe who will write the group's responses on the chart. Distribute one chart and one book to each group. Announce that before reading the book the children are to examine each illustration and to discuss what the character is doing. Explain that after the group shares its thoughts about the character, the scribe records the group's responses to the three questions. Each group hangs its chart for the class to examine during the next few days. Later, the groups might switch books, repeat the activity, and then compare their thoughts to the previous groups' responses.

Provide time for the groups to discuss personal experiences that were similar to the characters' experiences. Invite the children to write an individual account of what each thinks the group's story was about and to share their writings with other group members. Ask each group to compose a letter to the character telling what the children liked or disliked about the events portrayed, or to write a letter to the illustrator explaining what they think about his or her illustrative style. The class might start an adjective chart for character traits that are admired or disapproved of.

Bonnie Ivener, Albuquerque Public Schools and University of New Mexico

| WHO SAYS?

L ooking at point of view in children's books gives students the opportunity to use not only language skills but also critical thinking skills. Telling a story from a point of view different from that of the author is an interesting activity; using a wordless picture book to study point of view can require even more thought and imagination.

When selecting the book, match its complexity to the levels and experiences of your students. You might select a book such as *Hiccup* by Mercer Mayer (Dial, 1976) because it has only two characters and the story line is simple and direct. Two hippopotamuses go out on a picnic and ride in a rowboat. The male, elegant in his straw hat, tries to help the female get over the hiccups, and succeeds only when he pushes her out of the boat. Success makes him smug; she is disdainful. Then he gets the hiccups, and she gets her chance for revenge. There are only two points of view to compare, and all of the interaction is between these two characters.

A more complex story would be Mercer Mayer's *Frog Goes to Dinner* (Dial, 1974). It is the story of a frog who hides in a boy's pocket when the boy and his family go out to dinner. Once inside the restaurant, the frog creates all sorts of havoc, resulting in the family's being thrown out of the restaurant. The boy and frog both appear dejected, at least until they are in the bedroom with the door closed. Then both burst into laughter.

Sixteen characters are in this book (not counting nonparticipants such as restaurant patrons who only watch the action), and thus there are at least sixteen possible points of view for students to examine and develop. In addition, some of the characters witness only certain incidents, which means students could compare viewpoints or produce a joint retelling of the story by different characters.

Once a picture book is chosen, share it first with no purpose in mind but students' enjoyment and understanding. You might decide to share it in small groups, to let students take turns looking at the book, to obtain several copies of the book to pass around, or even to show a filmstrip or motion picture version of the book.

Then ask students to select one of the characters in the book and to imagine that they are that character as they look at the book for a second time. Next, students write what happened from the point of view of that character, including not only descriptions of the action but also what they think the character thought and felt about the events.

When students have finished writing and revising, several volunteers can read their writings aloud. Ask the listeners to talk about how the versions differed and why. This discussion can be followed by an exploration of why people sometimes perceive the same things differently, of the effect of an author's choice of point of view, and of the role and importance of various characters within a story.

Joan I. Glazer, Providence, Rhode Island

LITERATURE GROUPS
Intensive and Extensive Reading

WHY

Reading is a meaning-making process; learning to read is developmental and occurs over time. Select books on the basis of children's interest and the potential the books hold for making meaning that is personal to the children and in keeping with the author's intent. Read or skim through all books before selecting them for the classroom. To create an environment that is conducive to reading and that supports student initiative, select books that are an extension of the students' previous experiences with literature, their desire to know, and their reading abilities. Very young readers may need familiar stories with a high degree of predictability.

HOW

Select Books
The following books are appropriate for younger students. They were introduced during the first two months of school in Marilyn Harris Andres's first-grade classroom at Lee School, Columbia, Missouri:

Susan Blair, *The Three Billy Goats Gruff*
Norman Bridwell, *Kangaroo Stew*
Margaret Wise Brown, *Goodnight Moon*
Carolyn Burke and Jerome Harste, *All Kinds of Cats*
Polly Cameron, *I Can't Said the Ant*
Eric Carle, *The Very Hungry Caterpillar*
Bernadine Cook, *The Little Fish That Got Away*
Douglas F. Davis, *The Lion's Tail*
Paul Galdone, *The Little Red Hen; The Three Bears; The Three Little Pigs*
Janet L. Goss and Jerome C. Harste, *It Didn't Frighten Me*
Jerome Harste and Carolyn Burke, *Animal Babies*
Beth Hazel and Jerome Harste, *Icky Picky Sister*
Ezra Jack Keats, *Over in the Meadow*
Ruth Krauss, *The Carrot Seed*
Alan Mills and Rose Bonne, *I Know an Old Lady*
Phoebe Moore, *The Missing Necklace*
Maurice Sendak, *Chicken Soup with Rice*
Sharon K. Thomas and Marjorie Siegal, *No Baths for Tabatha*
Justin Wagner, *The Bus Ride*
Margot Zemach, *The Little Tiny Woman*

Books for older students might be selected from the following list. These books were introduced during the school year in Suzanne Davis's fifth-grade classroom at Lee School, Columbia, Missouri:

Louisa May Alcott, *Little Women*
Lloyd Alexander, *The Black Cauldron; The High King; Taran Wanderer*
Clyde Robert Bulla, *Shoeshine Girl*
Betsy C. Byers, *The Summer of the Swans; The Cybil War*
Beverly Cleary, *Ralph S. Mouse*
Vera Cleaver and Bill Cleaver, *Where the Lilies Bloom*
James Lincoln Collier and Christopher Collier, *My Brother Sam Is Dead*
Margaret Davidson, *Helen Keller's Teacher*
Marguerite de Angeli, *The Door in the Wall: Story of Medieval London*
Barthe DeClements, *Nothing's Fair in Fifth Grade*
Jeannette Eyerly, *The Seeing Summer*
Paula Fox, *The One-Eyed Cat*
Kenneth Grahame, *The Wind in the Willows*
Madeleine L'Engle, *A Wrinkle in Time*
C. S. Lewis, *The Lion, the Witch, and the Wardrobe; Prince Caspian*
Jack London, *The Call of the Wild*
Jane O'Connor, *Yours Till Niagara Falls, Abby*

Scott O'Dell, *Island of the Blue Dolphins*
Katherine Paterson, *Bridge to Terabithia; The Great Gilly Hopkins;*
    Jacob Have I   Loved
Wilson Rawls, *Where the Red Fern Grows*
Willo Davis Roberts, *The Girl with the Silver Eyes*
Marilyn Singer, *Tarantulas on the Brain*
Doris Buchanan Smith, *A Taste of Blackberries*
Elizabeth G. Speare, *The Witch of Blackbird Pond*
J. R. R. Tolkien, *The Hobbit*
Jules Verne, *Around the World in Eighty Days*

Form Groups

Introduce five or six books to the students with a brief discussion of the title, author, plot, and characters. Invite the children, on the basis of their own backgrounds of experience, to select a title. Challenge students to explore new genres and subjects, thereby giving them practice at making meaning in unexplored territory.

The children form groups, depending on their first or second choice of books. There should be no more than seven or eight children in a group.

Read the Books—Extensive Reading

Assign a substantial number of pages to read, with the understanding that the children may read beyond the assigned number if they wish. Students are expected to read, read, read! "Living" the meaning and being one with the action are encouraged.

Students are invited to keep records of their reading and to make brief reactions to their reading in a journal or reading log. Compiling a personal literary history by exploring literary worlds is the chief goal of extensive reading. Reading independently, the children expand their knowledge of the world, its people, and what it means to be human.

Read the Books—Intensive Reading

Intensive reading is practiced in literature study groups, where students who have read the same book come together to study and discuss the book. To begin, encourage the students to share their impressions, ideas, and problems encountered in constructing meaning from the text.

When a topic surfaces that holds a common interest and has the potential for altering perceptions, shift the discussion from sharing to dialogue, a joint undertaking that encompasses critical thinking. Through dialogue in the literature study groups, the teacher and students work with one another to disclose and to construct meaning, thereby expanding the potential meaning of the text. Dialogue that draws on the elements of story is the chief means through which the intensive study of literature is conducted. It is not necessary to hammer away at the elements of literature or narrate their meaning. The elements surface naturally as the discussion focuses on the way the characters cope, the mood of a story, the ordering of time, the creation of place, the development of character, the story structure, and the use of language and symbols.

It is through dialogue that students learn to construct meaning and to practice this process. Dialogue slows down the process, externalizing the act of meaning construction, and confirms that the meaning a reader brings to a text is every bit as important as the text itself. Together, as a shared experience, readers reflect on the importance of events that pull the story forward, the meaning of symbols, the significance of place, the development of character, and how the structure contributes to meaning development. With practice, students learn to seize meaning, to project it into the dialogue, and to benefit from insights and perspectives of their own making and of the author's making as well.

Ralph L. Peterson, Arizona State University, Tempe

BRIDGING THE GENERATIONS

Helping Students Understand the Elderly

Books can be valuable tools in fostering understanding. As you search for ways to help students identify with and appreciate the elderly, you may find the following annotated bibliography useful.

All of the books listed here present children and young people in close relationships with older people. Despite the difficult lessons they must learn, such as how to deal with the death of a grandfather or how to help a grandmother regain her independence, the characters in these stories openly celebrate their friendships with the older people they know. To help your students do the same, supplement the reading of one or more of these books with simple activities such as those appearing later in this article. When expanded and tailored to the needs of your students, the activities should work well in conjunction with any of the books read and will further your students' understanding of some of the special problems that older people face.

Nonna by Jennifer Bartoli (Harvey House, 1975). A garden and a cookie recipe remind a young boy of his grandmother, Nonna.

Nana Upstairs and Nana Downstairs by Tomi de Paola (Penguin Books, 1978). A small boy enjoys his relationship with his grandmother and his great-grandmother, but he learns to face their inevitable deaths.

Now One Foot, Now the Other by Tomi de Paola (Putnam, 1981). After his grandfather suffers a massive stroke, Bobby helps his grandfather learn to talk and walk again by using the saying "Now one foot, now the other."

Nana by Lyn Littlefield Hoopes (Harper and Row, 1982). Although her grandmother has died, a young girl still sees this important woman in all things living and growing around her.

My Grandpa Retired Today by Elaine Knox-Wagner; edited by Kathleen Tucker (Albert Whitman, 1982). Margery comes to a farewell party at the barbershop where her grandfather has worked for years. Sensing her grandpa's depression, she cheers him up by looking to the future when they'll have time to do all the things that he had been too busy to do before.

Through Grandpa's Eyes by Patricia MacLachlan (Harper and Row, 1980). Although John's grandpa is blind, a special relationship is inspired when he discovers the preciousness of   life and the beauty of nature through his grandfather's keenly developed senses.

Love My Grandma by Steven Palay (Raintree, 1977). An unnamed young girl describes the moments that she and her grandmother share together when her parents are out during the day.

Allison's Grandfather by Linda Peavy (Scribner, 1981). Erica thinks about the death of her friend Allison's grandfather and remembers the weekends they spent on his ranch together before he died.

When Grandpa Died by Margaret Stevens (Children's Press, 1979). A young girl tries to come to terms with the death of her grandfather.

References used to compile this list include: *Children's Books in Print* (Bowker); *Children's Catalog,* 14th ed. (Wilson, 1980, 1982); *The Bookfinder: A Guide to Children's Literature about the Needs and Problems of Youth Aged 2–15* (American Guidance Service, 1977); *Subject Guide to Books in Print* (Bowker, 1981, 1982).

SUGGESTED ACTIVITIES

1. Ask an older acquaintance or a grandparent of one of the students to read the book that students are reading and then to visit the class and join in a class discussion of the emotions and situations presented in the book.

2. Either before or after reading, invite an older person whom you know or a grandparent of one of the students to talk about how he or she feels about growing older. Ask this older person to explain feelings that are the same as those experienced when he or she was the same age as the students in the class, and feelings that are different. Allow students to ask questions about things they wonder about or worry about when they think of growing old.

3. Before reading one of the books that deals with a special problem faced by older people, form discussion groups and ask students to list and discuss some of the problems that they think they will face as they approach old age. After reading, ask students to form the same groups and to talk in more detail about the particular problem dealt with in the story.

4. After reading, divide the class into pairs of students and ask each pair to choose one of the dialogues in the book between the young person and the older person, to become familiar with the situation and emotions of the scene, and to act out the scene in their own words for the class.

5. Before reading, ask students to write a paragraph or two on how they think they will feel about themselves when they grow old. After reading, ask students if reading about the older person in the book changed their opinions at all and, if so, in what way.

6. Either before or after reading, invite a local physician to visit the class and talk about the process and effects of aging.

7. Before reading, brainstorm a list of specific problems that older people might have to face and then brainstorm a list of ways in which young people can help older people with these problems. After reading, ask students whether the main character helped the older person in the story. If so, how? If students think not, ask them if there might be some way that the main character could have helped. How?

8. After reading, discuss how the older character in the book spends most of his or her time. Ask students if they can imagine what this character might have done or been like twenty or thirty years previously. How would he or she have been different? Then invite several older people to visit the class and talk about ways they spend their time, what their hobbies are, and what the difference is between

how they currently spend their time and how they spent it twenty or thirty years ago.

FILMS IN THE CLASSROOM

To further help students develop a positive understanding of the elderly, consider the use of films as classroom resources. You may want to preview (for just the cost of the return postage), rent, or purchase award-winning films that deal with aging in our society. For information and to request a free film catalog, contact Learning Corporation of America at their toll-free number (1-800-323-6301) or, from Illinois, Alaska, or Hawaii, call collect: 1-312-940-1260. Additional films are available from Coronet/MTI Films, distributors of Learning Corporation of America. For information and to request their free catalog, call their toll-free number (1-800-621-2131) or, from Illinois, Alaska, or Hawaii, call collect: 1-312-940-1260. (From these locations, the collect number is the same for the two companies.)

Maria Valeri-Gold, Marietta, Georgia

ENRICHING READING
Some Resources

Children are natural poets. They love to play with words. Share with them your favorite books of poetry and a genuine sense of excitement. Encourage their experimenting with words as they learn how to use their language. Stress that poems do not need to rhyme and that feelings, imagery, meaning, and a musical quality of sound are far more important achievements.

There are many good books for introducing poetry to children. A good anthology can provide a variety of poems and poetic forms. Once the groundwork has been laid, it is time to experience what poetry can do for children. Let a poem stir the senses and tap the emotional depths. Here poetry wins—hands down—over prose.

For the pure enjoyment of a hearty laugh, you can't go wrong with Shel Silverstein's *Where the Sidewalk Ends* (Harper and Row, 1974) and *A Light in the Attic* (Harper and Row, 1981). The former is a longtime favorite of the kindergarten crowd, while the latter has been on The New York Times best-sellers list so long that the weeks blend into years.

In a more serious vein, there is the poetry of Langston Hughes in *Don't You Turn Back* (Alfred Knopf, 1969) and a little picture book by Alan Brightman called *Like Me* (Little, Brown, 1976), which teach human values through poetry without preaching. If your students are emotionally and intellectually ready, you can provide a glimpse of life in a concentration camp through the poetry and artwork of the children of Terezin. These poems and drawings, miraculously hidden from the children's Nazi captors, were unearthed after the war and published in *I Never Saw Another Butterfly,* edited by Hand Volavkova (Schocken Books, 1974).

For actual teaching ideas, nothing beats *Wishes, Lies, and Dreams* (Harper and Row, 1970) and *Rose, Where Did You Get That Red?* (Vintage Books, 1974) by Kenneth Koch. Developed by Koch while working with New York City public school children, these poetry ideas channel children's natural energy and give form to their inner thoughts and feelings. Koch encourages them to play with unconventional imagery and incongruity.

One of the poetry ideas in *Wishes, Lies, and Dreams* that I have used successfully with writers of all ages is "I used to . . . . / but now I . . . ." I usually ask students to bring from home something they used as a baby. These mementos of early childhood are used to prompt students' poems. Another favorite writing pattern is Koch's "I seem to be . . . . / but really I am . . . ." Here are excerpts from poems written by my students using these patterns:

> *I used to play with letter blocks,*
> *But now I play with computers.*
>
> *I seem to be a person with no problems,*
> *But really I am a person with her problems filed alphabetically.*

Whether you use the poems and writing activities suggested here or select favorites of your own, make sure to share with your students your excitement and pleasure in reading poetry. Issue them an invitation, as Shel Silverstein did, to "come sit by my fire / For we have some flax-golden tales to spin."

Alice Ganz, Longwood Central School District, Suffolk County, New York

| WRITING HAIKU

PURPOSE

- To read and write haiku
- To select words carefully
- To be aware of a syllable and line pattern
- To write to create a mood

MATERIALS

- Books and filmstrips about haiku
- Clipboards, pads of paper, pencils

> *Yellow daffodil*
> *Gently swaying in spring breeze.*
> *Happy is my heart.*

With a little care, you can adapt the study of haiku to almost any grade level and still do justice to traditional elements of the art form. The poem above was written by a primary student during our study of haiku. As an extension of a unit on Japan, my students and I learned about the haiku form for one-half hour a day for a week.

On the first morning, I showed students a sound filmstrip entitled *Haiku* (from Pied Piper Production's Literature for Children series). On the chalkboard I listed some traditional characteristics of haiku:

- Contains very few words
- Is written in a special pattern composed of a first line of five syllables, a second line of seven syllables, and a third line of five syllables
- Has nature and the seasons as subject matter
- Captures the mood of a brief moment
- Evokes an emotional response in the reader

Then I read aloud selected haiku from the anthologies listed below. Though I read a greater number of traditional Japanese haiku, I also read several free-form, contemporary haiku by Japanese and American poets.

Haiku Vision in Poetry and Photography by Ann Atwood (Scribner, 1977).Suggested grade level: 4 and up.

Cricket Songs: Japanese Haiku, compiled and translated by Harry Behn (Harcourt Brace Jovanovich, 1964). Suggested grade level: 4–7.

Wind, Sand, and Sky by Rebecca Caudill; illustrated by Donald Carrick (Dutton, 1976). Suggested grade level: 1–6.

Birds, Frogs, and Moonlight, translated by Sylvia Cassedy and Kunihiro Suetake; illustrated by Vo-Dinh (Doubleday, 1967). Suggested grade level: 2–5.

Don't Tell the Scarecrow and Other Japanese Poems by Issa, Yayu, Kikaku, and other Japanese poets; illustrated by Talivaldis Stubis (Four Winds Press, 1969). Suggested grade level: K–4.

A Few Flies and I: Haiku by Issa, selected by Jean Merrill and Ronni Solbert from translations by R. H. Blyth and Nobuyuki Yuasa; illustrated by Ronni Solbert (Pantheon, 1969). Suggested grade level: 3–7.

Hello, Small Sparrow by Hannah Lyons Johnson; illustrated by Tony Chen (Lothrop, Lee and Shepard, 1971). Suggested grade level: 3–6.

In a Spring Garden, edited by Richard Lewis; illustrated by Ezra Jack Keats (Dial Press, 1965). Suggested grade level: K–7.

Flower Moon Snow by Kazue Mizumura (Crowell, 1977). Suggested grade level: K–4.

I See the Winds by Kazue Mizumura (Crowell, 1966). Suggested grade level: 2–5.

I showed students how to clap their hands in time to the reading of a poem in order to help them count syllables, but I stressed that following the pattern shouldn't be the most important consideration in writing their own haiku. Choosing words that sounded good together and that helped create the desired mood would be just as important.

The next morning, we looked at pictures of Japanese life that I had assembled, including study prints and pictures from magazines. I asked students, "What have you learned about Japan so far?" After hearing some of their ideas, I asked, "Do any of the things you've learned give you ideas for your own haiku poems?" Students' suggestions were listed on the chalkboard to help them decide on topics.

The third morning was warm, so we went outside and walked in the park next to the school. Students brought clipboards, pads of paper, and pencils so that they could write and edit their own haiku. We looked at the flowering trees and talked about the seasons and how we felt about them. When the students seemed ready, I asked them to put down some of their thoughts in haiku form.

On the last two days of the week, we spent our time reading aloud and discussing our poems. After a student read his or her poem, we would share our ideas about it. I posed these questions to the class:

What emotions do you feel after hearing this poem?
Which words in the poem do the most to create the mood?
Are there any words that don't fit in with the mood of the poem?
Which words do you think could be replaced with stronger ones?
What specific changes would you suggest to the poem's author? (At times students' suggestions led to a word change, but each poet had the final say and sometimes decided that he or she had already chosen the best word to fit the poem.)
Which traditional characteristics of a haiku does this poem have?
How closely does this poem fit the traditional pattern of lines and syllables? (With younger students you may want to relax the emphasis on form and omit this question and the previous one.)

Sometimes we spent part of our discussion time helping students find words that fit the pattern better. For example, Scott was trying to create an image of Pegasus, but his second line, "Born with wings to fly, flying" did not sound right to him. With the group's help, Scott came up with the following version:

White winged Pegasus
Born with wings to fly, soaring
Reaching for the stars.

When students had final versions ready, they dictated their poems to me, and I entered the poems on our word processor. I printed out their poems, gave each student a printed copy to take home, and kept one copy in the classroom. To create a class haiku book, the mother of one of the students copied each poem in calligraphy on a sheet of paper. The students were so pleased with their poems that they wanted to paint watercolors as accompaniments. We glued one watercolor onto each page of poetry, made a title page and a dedication page, and used grasscloth wallpaper for the cover. A black, silklike cord was used as a binding. But before we bound the book, I made enough photocopies so that each student could have his or her own haiku book.

Adapted from an idea by Marlene Lazzara, Henking School, Glenview, Illinois

3 | EMPHASIS: INTEGRATING THE LANGUAGE ARTS

PART 3

LEVERAGE

INTEGRATING THE

ENTERPRISE

WHERE DID THE BEAR GO?

WHY

To aid children's language development by having them predict what could happen in a given situation

WHO

Students in kindergarten through grade 2

HOW

Tape bear tracks made from construction paper or poster board in a path along the floor leading to a window in the classroom. When the students arrive in the classroom, ask them to look at the path of the tracks. Tell them a story, such as the one below, about how the bear got in the room and left the prints.

> Last night after we all went home, the janitor said he heard something walking around in the classrooms. He walked down the hall and looked in our classroom window, and there was a big brown grizzly bear. He became so frightened that he ran back up the hall and shut himself up in the broom closet. He kept waiting for the bear to leave, but he fell asleep and woke up just before school started this morning. He remembered the bear, so he rushed back down the hall. The bear was gone. All the janitor found were these bear tracks and an open window. What could have happened to the bear? What was it doing in our room? Where did it come from?

Let about five students at a time follow the bear path. Ask them to look for clues (such as overturned books and cans of food that you've placed in the classroom). Explain that the clues will help predict what happened to the bear. Each student is to follow the path without talking and to predict what happened. After everyone has followed the path and drawn conclusions, the children volunteer what they think happened to the bear. As they tell their versions, write their predictions on the chalkboard. When everyone has given an opinion, read aloud all the versions. The students might want to read the predictions together a second time.

WHAT ELSE

Have the class divide into groups to follow the bear tracks and to discuss the clues. Students in each group write a story about what happened to the bear. Compile the stories into a book for the class learning center or the library.

Reference

Rubin, Dorothy. *Teaching Elementary Language Arts*. 2nd ed. Holt, Rinehart and Winston, 1980.

Lesia R. Lawson, Bluefield College, Bluefield, Virginia, and Richland Elementary School, Richland, Virginia

LEARNING FROM A FEELY BOX

PURPOSE
- To compare and contrast familiar and unfamiliar textures
- To talk and write about textures

MATERIALS
- A "feely box" made from a half-gallon cardboard milk container or a shoe box with a lid
- Miscellaneous textures, such as a scrap of carpet, burlap, a woven basket, a fir twig, sand, rubber bands, marbles, etc.
- Magazines, scissors, tape or glue, paper, pencils, crayons

Begin by preparing a "feely box" into which a student can insert a hand and feel a texture without seeing the object. You can either open the top of a half-gallon cardboard milk container and cover the container with self-adhesive plastic paper (leaving the top open for the student's hand) or cut a hole in the side of a lidded shoe box. Place drawing and writing materials and the "feely box" on a table in the center of the room and post a class roster nearby.

As an introduction to describing textures, ask students to sit in a circle and close their eyes as you say, "Imagine that you are petting a baby bunny. Move your hand over the back of the bunny. Your fingertips are helping you feel the bunny. Now open your eyes and tell us what that bunny felt like." My students made these comments:

"My bunny's big."

"Mine's wiggly . . . and soft."

"Yeah, soft."

As students think of words, write them on the board. Point out that a number of different touch words can be used to describe the same texture.

Next, hold up the "feely box" and tell students that each will have the chance to close his or her eyes and feel the texture inside. You will place a different object in the "feely box" every day or two, or as long as student interest lasts. After a student feels the textured object in the box, he or she uses drawing materials from the center table and describes the texture, whether by writing descriptive words, drawing a picture of the texture, or cutting out and pasting magazine pictures that show a similar texture.

Students are responsible for putting checks by their names on the class roster after feeling each texture and for taping their response sheets up on the display board. When everyone's name is checked off, indicating that each person has felt an object, hold a class meeting to discuss all the responses and to open the "feely box" to see what's inside.

A three-ring notebook makes a handy permanent record of student descriptions. After the objects from the "feely box" are taped or glued onto pages, students can review the experience individually, read their own and classmates' descriptions, and look at the drawings they created to match the textures.

As a follow-up activity, students enjoy the challenge offered by Tana Hoban's *Look Again* (Macmillan, 1981). This book contains unusual photographs of textures of ordinary objects. It invites active discussion. You might also consider showing Scholastic Magazine's Beginning Concepts filmstrip,

Bumpy Lumpy, which presents ordinary objects and unusual texture words with lively music.

Ellen R. Smachetti, North Adams, Massachusetts

| POOH BEAR VISITS

WHY

- To familiarize students with a popular work of children's literature
- To encourage creative writing responses to a character in a story
- To promote letter writing

WHO

Students in kindergarten through grade 3

HOW

Introduce *Winnie the Pooh* by A. A. Milne by seating a stuffed Pooh Bear in a chair of honor in the classroom. On the board write a letter of introduction from Pooh informing the class that he will be visiting for awhile. Students will respond with many questions and much dialogue, and some will want to tell the class the Pooh stories that they know. Read aloud a favorite Pooh adventure and invite students to bring Pooh books and records from home or the library. Encourage students to write letters to Pooh. (I put a plastic pail under Pooh's chair with the word *Hunny* written on it. All letters went into the Hunny pot to be answered by Pooh Bear helpers—sometimes myself or a student teacher; sometimes other children.)

WHAT ELSE

The sky is the limit. Pooh visited our classroom for nine weeks. He taught us to make a healthy honey breakfast, honey candy, and a honey snack. We became food critics and came up with adjectives to describe recipes. Pooh wrote the whole class a letter each Monday and individual letters on Friday. We drew Pooh illustrations and wrote stories about our bears. Students brought other favorite stuffed animals to school, making our room an exciting animal land.

Lynne C. Moore, Springfield Public Schools, Missouri

THE GREAT COOKIE CHASE

Following Directions to Find The Gingerbread Boy

WHY

To give students practice in reading and following directions

WHO

Primary students

HOW

Read aloud to the class *The Gingerbread Boy*. (Any of the several versions currently in print will do.) Encourage students to talk about the story and to list main events in sequential order. If cooking facilities are available, ask students if they would like to bake their own Gingerbread Boy. Call for volunteers to bring ingredients from home. Enlist an adult volunteer to help on baking day.

Involve children in reading directions, measuring, mixing, and shaping on the day of baking. Students return to class while the Gingerbread Boy bakes. Before the children go back to the kitchen, the adult volunteer removes the Gingerbread Boy from the oven and hides him in a previously determined place somewhere in the building. A note is left in the kitchen that instructs the children to go to a certain location, where another note is found. Depending on the maturity of the students, they continue following directions until they reach the fourth or fifth place, where they find the Gingerbread Boy. Students may celebrate the discovery by eating the cookie.

WHAT ELSE

1. Students work individually or in groups to write a story about a cookie person.
2. Divide the class into small groups. Let each group hide a prize for another group and write a series of messages directing the students to the prize.

Beverly Simpson, Hannibal–La Grange College, Hannibal, Missouri

| BEES, BEES, BEES

WHY

- To extend students' oral language
- To integrate writing with reading
- To encourage class participation and involvement
- To help students learn about bees

WHO

Primary students

HOW

Day One

Begin by listing on chart paper questions that students have about bees. Read aloud a book about bees. Next, ask students to list new words or terms they heard, such as *honeycomb, drone, beekeeper, beeline, royal jelly, colony, queen, worker, cell, hive, proboscis,* or *tail-wagging dance.* Students then pair with a partner, choose a term from this list, and illustrate its meaning.

Keep a variety of books about bees, both factual and fictional, available for browsing, reading, and research. (A list of suggested titles appears at the end of the activity.) Some students might write and illustrate books about bees. The covers of the books can be made from black and yellow construction paper.

Day Two

Read aloud the poem "For the Love of Honey" by Sharen Scalena. Talk about the rhythm of this poem and ask students to name the rhyming words. Bring in a large loaf of bread and a jar of honey for students to spread on the bread. They'll need little encouragement to taste the honey. Make a language experience chart by asking students to list words that describe the honey, such as *sticky, sweet, yellow, gooey.*

Glue a "honey-shaped" piece of yellow construction paper to a larger piece of white or brown paper cut in the shape of a slice of bread. Invite students to write their impressions of honey on the yellow paper.

Day Three

Read aloud the poem "Wendy the Worker Bee" by Sharen Scalena. Read the poem several times so that students can enjoy the rhyme and rhythm of the words. Ask them to list the jobs Wendy disliked doing and what she would rather be doing instead of working. Then invite each student to complete the sentence "I am as busy as a bee when . . . " and to illustrate his or her response.

Day Four

Read aloud and enjoy "Claire the Bear" by Sharen Scalena, perhaps as a choral reading. Ask students to talk about why the bees were going to chase Claire home. Explain how most of us obtain our honey from a grocery store or a beekeeper, rather than collecting it from a beehive. Then have students, working in small groups, prepare Peanut Honey Candy from the following recipe: mix together 1 cup peanut butter, 1 cup honey, 1 cup powdered milk, 1/2 teaspoon vanilla, and 1/2 cup peanuts; shape into bite-sized balls.

Day Five

Read aloud *Fire! Fire! Said Mrs. McGuire* by Bill Martin, Jr. Ask students to write a group bee story patterned after the book. One class wrote the following story.

"Bees, Bees!" said Mrs. Cheese.
"Where, Where?" said Mr. Care.

"In the beehive," said Mr. Brive.
"In the cell," said Mr. Bell.
"Underground," said Mr. Brown.
"What a stinger!" said Mrs. Binger.
"Help, Help!" said Mrs. Belp.
"Beekeeper, Beekeeper!" yelled Mrs. Reepeeper.
"Safe and sound!" said Mr. Bound.

Students then choose a phrase from the group story or the original story and illustrate it for a class book or wall mural.

Day Six
Invite a beekeeper to school to describe his or her job and to display the necessary clothing and equipment. Students then share their illustrations, charts, and books about bees, read aloud the bee poems, and serve the Peanut Honey Candy. Afterward, they write thank-you notes to the beekeeper for speaking to the class about bees.

SUGGESTED READING LIST

Barton, Byron. *Buzz, Buzz, Buzz*. Macmillan, 1973.
Goudey, Alice E. *Here Come the Bees*. Scribner, 1960.
Lecht, June. *Honey Bees*. National Geographic Society, 1973.
Neal, Charles. *What Is a Bee?* Benefic Press, 1961.
Scalena, Sharen. *Reading Experiences in Science Series: Bees*. Peguis Publishers, 1980.
Swenson, Valerie. *Bees and Wasps*. Maxton Publishing, n.d.
Teale, Edwin W. *The Bees*. Children's Press, 1967.
Tibbets, Albert. *First Book of Bees*. Watts, 1952.

Mary A. Evans, Columbia Public Schools, Missouri

WHAT'S HAPPENING HERE?

WHY

The abilities to observe and describe are prerequisite skills for making meaning of process-oriented learning experiences, including scientific processes and aesthetic experiences such as art, music, and literature studies. Effective problem-solving and decision-making abilities in the social, political, and economic worlds are grounded in accurate observation and description. It is important for students to distinguish among and accurately describe phenomena or events, inferences, and personal reactions or feelings. Through involvement in the activities in this unit, children will have the opportunity to:

- Demonstrate a variety of ways to observe (touch, taste, smell, hear, see)
- Demonstrate a variety of ways to describe (oral descriptions, written descriptions, bar and line graphs, charts, lists, drama, pantomime, models, drawings)
- Develop vocabulary for descriptions, observations, inferences, and feelings
- Distinguish among observations, inferences, and feelings
- Be able to describe events in terms of the sequence in which they occur
- Be able to make decisions based on observations

WHO

All elementary students

HOW

Sensory Maze

Make a maze for students to walk through barefoot and blindfolded. Include such objects as ice, cooked noodles, wet mud, water, dry cereal, or other tactile objects. Have students walk through the maze one by one, using their hands or feet to feel their way through. Then ask the still-blindfolded students to infer or guess what they walked through and to name the properties that identified the objects, such as "It was ice because it was cold."

Explain to students that they are inferring what was there by how it felt and that they need to use other senses to be certain. Ask what other senses they could use. Ask students to go back through the maze, this time observing with their eyes also. Then they discuss properties of the objects that they saw with their eyes.

Next, ask children to describe what they saw by making a map of the maze on which they label each item they saw and felt. Students might also write about what they observed in the maze with their eyes, hands, and feet. The following questions might stimulate their writing:

What did we observe?
What did I first think it was?
How did it feel?
How did it look?

Do You Want It?

Fill a plastic gallon juice or milk container with water, red food coloring, and pure lemon juice; the liquid should look like red Kool-Aid. Blindfold children and ask them to sit in a circle. Tell them that you are holding a mystery object. Do they want it? Explain that you will give them clues to observe with their various senses so that they can infer what the object is and can decide if they want it.

1. Shake the jug. Ask children if they want it. Why? What properties does it have? List the properties on the chalkboard.
2. Walk around and let children feel the jug. Ask if they want it. Why? What properties does it have? Make a second list.
3. Children remove their blindfolds and see the jug. Ask if they want it. Why? What properties does it have? Make a third list and review the characteristics on the three lists.
4. Pass the jug around and let children smell the beverage. Ask if they want it. Why? What properties does it have? Make a fourth list, again reviewing the other lists.
5. Give everyone a taste of the beverage. Ask if they want it. Why? What properties does it have? Make a fifth list and review the other lists.

Discuss what happened and why. Make a chart that lists all the ways they observed: hearing, feeling, seeing, smelling, tasting. Make a chart that lists the way they inferred (by guessing, by thinking, and so on). Make a chart that lists the words used to describe (it smells like, it feels like, it looks like, and so on). Make a chart that lists ways to describe. On all of these charts include columns so that you or students can check off daily when they use a particular sense and when they use a particular way of describing.

WHAT ELSE

Continue to stimulate students' abilities at observation and description with the following activities.

Can You Guess What I See?

Demonstrate a guessing game by placing an object behind a barrier (perhaps in a box). Describe the object's properties and then ask the children to guess what the object is. After you've repeated the procedure with several objects, point out how important the students' descriptions are. They must describe all properties before they can make a guess.

Pair children with partners and ask them to describe an object, such as a cup, an ear of corn, a clock, or a ball. Emphasize that they cannot say what the object does—they are to describe the properties they observe. After students have described several objects, discuss the activity with them. Mark the charts for types of observing, inferring, and describing. Ask children to write about the activity in their observation books. Encourage their writing by asking questions about what they observed.

Object Tray

Fill a tray with a variety of unrelated objects. Divide the class into three teams. Tell each team that they will see the tray for one minute and then are to list all the objects they remember seeing. Students discuss their lists and learn how well they do at observing. Students then mark the charts and report the activity in their observation notebooks.

As an additional activity, ask each team in turn to classify the objects on the tray. They are to observe characteristics that are similar, such as all metal or all red objects. Students list and discuss their categories.

Mirrors

Pass out mirrors and ask children to observe themselves. Invite them to describe themselves by making a picture and a written description for their notebooks. Students mark on the charts the type of observations and description that they used.

Tasting Tray

Fill a tray with a variety of foods and invite students to taste the items. Graph on a bar graph their observations, such as *sweet, salty, sour, tasteless*. Make a separate graph for each child so that everyone can insert a graph in his or her observation notebook.

Celery Stalk

As children observe, place a celery stalk with leaves in a jar filled with water and food coloring. Discuss the procedure and ask students to report their observations as a separate chapter in their observation notebooks. They are to observe this plant daily and to record their observations. When the color starts moving upward, encourage children to measure it and record its progress. They make a line graph in their notebooks and fill it in daily. Encourage discussion throughout the experiment.

What Sound Is It?

Behind a barrier, make a sound and ask children to infer what the sound was. Then display the object. Discuss if they had enough information from the sound alone to observe what the object was. Students write up the activity in their observation notebooks.

Pantomime

Invite an older student, a parent, or another student to pantomime an activity, such as putting on a raincoat or planting a row of beans. Children observe and describe the pantomime, and then guess what activity was being demonstrated. In the discussion that follows, students may want to imitate the pantomime. They report on the activity in their notebooks and keep charts up to date.

Observation of Feelings

Arrange for another person to run into the room as if there were an emergency or as if something has angered or upset this person. Dramatize a series of events that would create a stressful situation.

When the crisis is over, tell children it was just a drama and ask for their reactions. List how they felt and what feelings they observed: fear, anger, humor, or another emotion. Encourage students to re-create the drama in sequence, explaining that this is a way to describe what happened. The class writes a group story of the event. Type and duplicate copies of the story so that students can add it to their notebooks.

Sandra Lee Smith, Phoenix Elementary School District #1, Arizona, and Willard Kniep, Global Perspectives in Education, New York, New York

GROW A UNIT (FROM TURNIPS)

WHY

A major underlying principle in planning language arts activities is that we want students to sense the wholeness of language, as one use of language grows naturally from another and leads to yet another. Too frequently, in contrast, children leave elementary school perceiving, albeit unconsciously, that the language arts are a random collection of isolated, unrelated activities. Using a book as a seed, we can grow an array of related activities, emphasizing the connectedness of the various language arts, as parts of a plant are connected to each other. The following description of a teaching unit is provided to show a process that teachers could use with many other books.

WHO

All elementary students

HOW

Begin with an observing and describing activity to help develop children's abilities to use language for these two thinking purposes. A significant way we learn is by seeing how an unfamiliar person, place, object, or experience is like or unlike those we've encountered before. To foster such comparing and contrasting, bring a bunch of turnips, tops and all, to class. Encourage children to use their eyes to note color, shape, size; their fingers to note contrasting texture, resistance; their noses to note the varying smells of roots and greens. Then cut into the turnip so that the children can taste what is probably an unfamiliar vegetable. All the descriptive words students suggest may be listed on the chalkboard in categories according to the sense involved. Help children see that some descriptive words fit into more than one category—for example, some textures can be seen as well as felt. In the process, we are moving from sensory impressions to words, which will later be shaped into factual accounts of the activity.

Maintain the turnip theme by reading aloud *The Three Little Pigs,* a story in which turnips are integral. (I've found useful the versions by Lorinda Cauley and by Erik Blegvad.) Encourage the children to contribute their observations about the story line, the vocabulary used, and the nature of the illustrations. As students listen to each other and observe the teacher recording their comments in a list on the board, they have an opportunity to see the interrelatedness of the language arts. Again we are moving from sensory impressions through oral language into written language, as children may later follow up this step with compositions describing which of the versions they prefer and why.

The Cauley and Blegvad versions of *The Three Little Pigs* are effective since they offer some readily observable differences in language and visuals. There are myriad versions of the story available; in addition to differences in the text and illustrations, some also offer significant plot variations. The two editions recommended here include the trips to pick apples, harvest turnips, and visit the fair, details that are omitted in some other versions. With older children who can read fluently, four or more versions could be used as students meet in small groups to read a version aloud, analyze it, and report back to the entire class.

Include informal classroom drama activities with this unit. Many activities in this story can be mimed: the pigs building their houses, pulling turnips and picking apples, examining the churn maker's booth at the fair, and selecting a churn. There are also plenty of scenes for student-generated dialogues: the distraught mother pig bidding her sons farewell, the devious wolf beguiling the pig into going apple picking, the clever pig explaining his use of the churn to elude the wolf. Follow up the mimes and dialogues by inviting the children to write a narrative to link the scenes together in their own words. Then, put the various scenes in sequence and share the improvised presentations with other children to encourage their observing and listening skills.

WHAT ELSE

1. Follow a suggestion offered by James Moffet and Betty J. Wagner (1983). In classes of older students, the student observers can take notes during the presentations and then write up their observations as factual accounts.
2. Other oral activities grow naturally: storytelling can follow watching a filmed version of *The Three Little Pigs.* (You might show the animated version by Disney Productions or a film using live animals, available from Cornet Instructional Films.) Let children view the film with the sound turned off, and tape-record their descriptions of the events. Students can illustrate some of the events in the story,

working either in groups or individually. Then the illustrations can be shared with younger students while they listen to the taped versions of the tale.

3. Writing experiences evolve easily from this story. Read the book to the point at which the wolf is threatening to jump down the chimney. Even if the children already know the usual ending, invite them to brainstorm as many other endings as they can think of. Generating ideas can serve as a prewriting experience, and the children can select from these ideas in later compositions. You might have each child choose one of the characters and rewrite the story from the point of view of that character. A group discussion can prepare students for writing these narratives. Some sample questions follow:

> What were the mother pig's misgivings as she sent her children into the world?
> How could the first two pigs have been so gullible while their sibling was more aware of what might happen?
> Why didn't the wolf anticipate a trap in the chimney?

Recasting a third-person narration into a first-person account helps children become aware of their own ethnocentrism and begin to explore, orally or in writing, the reasons why characters do certain things, how they feel about what they do, and what happens to them.

4. Try a story extension with your class. Invite students to write about what the third pig did the day after dining on boiled wolf. Introduce them to the assignment by asking such questions as "Where did the third pig go the following day? Whom did he meet? What did they do?" Arrange for students to read their stories to children in a younger class. Such cross-grade sharing provides a tangible audience for any writing task. This activity gives older students the opportunity to respond to and write about classic tales a second time, and students in the intermediate grades enjoy tales that they or the teacher might initially consider too juvenile.

5. But such an integrated unit need not be based only on traditional tales. If you're hungry, try growing a unit: lots of books contain seeds. For example, plant *Avocado Baby* by John Burningham in your classroom and see how it grows. It's a thoroughly charming, though somewhat improbable, contemporary tale of a puny baby who gathers extraordinary strength from eating an avocado. Many other children's books provide such organic opportunities as described here. Your language arts program will gather strength as you grow into wholeness from such books as these and others that you can locate and nurture into a flourishing unit.

Work Cited

Moffet, James, and Betty J. Wagner. *Student-Centered Language Arts and Reading, K–13*. 3d ed. Houghton Mifflin, 1983.

John Warren Stewig, University of Wisconsin–Milwaukee

LATE BLOOMERS

Leo, *the Late Bloomer* by Robert Kraus (Simon and Schuster, 1971) is a story about a young tiger who can't do anything right. He can't read. He can't write. He can't draw. He is a sloppy eater. And he never says a word. Leo's mother assures his concerned father that Leo is just a late bloomer. Leo's father watches for signs of blooming, but although the seasons come and go, it seems Leo will not bloom. In his own good time, however, Leo does read, and write, and draw, and eat neatly. He also speaks—and it's not just a word, it's a whole sentence: "I made it!" The illustrations—bold, playful watercolors—add to the story's appeal. Here are some ideas for discussion and writing:

1. Talk about what it means to say a person has "bloomed." Ask students to think of some ways in which they have bloomed—for example, growing taller, learning to ride a bike, making new friends. Describe to students the ways in which you have bloomed at certain points in your own life.
2. Read the story aloud again, asking students to notice how differently Leo's mother and his father act toward him. Ask students to suggest reasons for each parent's actions. Then ask students to write letters to Leo's father explaining why he shouldn't worry about Leo.
3. Help students tape their index and middle fingers together. Then ask them to try to do simple tasks such as tying their shoes, writing their names, or buttoning buttons. Tape your own index and middle fingers together and try the same tasks, too.

Ask students how they feel when they can't do something that they try to do. Point out that everyone finds certain tasks more difficult than others. Discuss what activities each student feels good at, and which activities each student would like to do better. Ask students, "Are there things that your best friend or your brother or sister can't do as well as you? What could you say to make your friend or your brother or sister feel better about not being as good at these activities?"

4. After students have read and discussed the book, say, "Suppose that once Leo starts to 'bloom,' he realizes that he can learn to do anything he wants to do. What do you think he would decide to learn?" After students have offered ideas, suggest that students pretend to be newspaper reporters twenty years from now, writing a newspaper story about Leo and all that he has learned to do in the last twenty years. Students may invent imaginary interviews with Leo in which he explains how he felt about being a late bloomer and how he feels now, and in which Leo gives advice to other late bloomers.

Pat Friedli, Nancy Dean, and Barb Burwell, Mount Pleasant, Michigan

TROLL TALES
Cumulative Literary Experiences

WHO

Students in grades 1–2

WHY

Cognitive psychologists have demonstrated that the quality of comprehension is determined, to a great extent, by the prior knowledge or schemata that the readers/listeners bring to the text. That is, readers/listeners generate meaning by bringing their knowledge of the world, language, and literature to the text and by building bridges between existing schema or prior knowledge and the new information in the text.

Recent studies of literacy development have also examined the interrelationships between reading and writing. After a review of the findings from correlational and experimental studies on reading/writing relationships, Sandra Stotsky concluded that "reading experience seems to be a consistent correlate of, or influence on, writing ability. Thus, it is possible that reading experience may be as critical a factor in developing writing ability as writing instruction itself " (Stotsky 1983, 637).

OBJECTIVES

1. In this activity the children will be invited to respond to each new literary selection in light of previous literary experiences. They will learn strategies for reactivating relevant background knowledge and for making connections between prior literary experiences and present ones, and they will learn to apply these strategies as they read independently.
2. The children will learn to use their literary background as a natural resource for composing their own narratives.
3. The children will move out from literature into drama, art, dance, and music in order to reconstruct or translate literary experiences into other forms of communication.

HOW

Building Literary Background and Making Connections

Read aloud *Trolls* by Ingri and Edgar d'Aulaire to introduce children to the world of trolls and their relatives. Ask the children to use the information in this book to generate a list of troll characteristics and habits as well as myths about encounters between trolls and humans. This list is recorded on chart paper, and it serves as the base from which to begin subsequent excursions into the troll world. Place a display table or shelf near the troll chart to hold the collection of troll tales that provide the literary context for this language arts activity sequence. (A suggested reading list of troll tales appears at the end of the activity.) Read several of the books aloud to the class and encourage the children to select one or more of these books to read independently or with a partner.

During the class story sessions, ask the children to consider each new story in light of those read or heard previously. That is, ask them to look for connections between the diverse tales in the troll collection. Guide this search by introducing questions into the class discussion of each story. These questions also serve as a model for self-questioning during independent reading. Below are examples of questions that can be used to stimulate children's comprehension.

1. What troll information found in the d'Aulaires's *Trolls* can also be found in this story?
2. What information is different than that found in the d'Aulaires's *Trolls*? How would you explain these differences?
3. What new information about trolls is included in this story and should be added to our wall chart about trolls and their relatives?
4. Authors have many different ways to tell a story. That is, they have different styles of writing. Compare this story with one or two other troll tales. What is special about the way each tale is told?
5. Artists also have many different ways to illustrate a story. That is, they have different styles of painting, drawing, and so forth. Look at the illustrations in three of the troll tales in our collection. How are they similar or different? Does each artist seem to have a special style?
6. What magic powers do trolls use against human characters?
7. In what ways do trolls respond to those who please them? Which trolls seem to have kind hearts? What clues in the stories help you answer this question?
8. What are some of the tricks used by human characters to outwit troll characters?
9. Which stories teach a lesson? Explain.

In this language arts sequence, the children undergo cumulative literary experiences in which they listen to, read, and compare the troll tales. Then they are invited to compose their own troll tales.

Using Literary Background as a Context for Composition

In preparation for the writing experience, invite the children to study the wall chart while one child reads aloud what has been recorded about trolls. By this time new items have been added to the original list, just as the children have been adding to their own growing store of troll knowledge. Then the children briefly review each of the troll tales read by individuals or heard in the group sessions. This review of the troll literature sets the stage for composition by reactivating and organizing information associated with prior reading experiences. The children bring their "troll schema" to the process of composing a troll tale.

To make the children feel comfortable about engaging in this independent writing assignment, reassure them that invented spelling is acceptable in their initial drafts. Some will find that drawing a picture of their story idea prior to translating it into written language is a helpful way to get started. Others will prefer to do the writing first and a picture later. Those whose literacy skills are very limited and who appear threatened by this assignment might dictate their story ideas to you or to an older student for transcription onto paper.

Children who are writing independently may be paired with a partner. During the course of the writing process, writers share their stories-in-progress with their partners and receive feedback. These writing-partner interactions are intended to help the children become aware of their potential readers and to become critical readers of their own writing.

As children complete their first drafts, they meet with the teacher to share their stories and to discuss necessary corrections and revisions. The final stories and accompanying illustrations are bound into individual books and read aloud to the whole class. Each book remains in the troll tale collection on display in the classroom and later is taken home.

WHAT ELSE

To culminate the troll sequence, invite the children to select one of the tales from the troll collection and to recreate it through drama, dance, music, or art. The children may choose to work independently, with a partner, or with a small group to produce a play, a mural, a puppet show, a dance, a song, a poem, or other form of creative expression that would provide a format for recreating favorite troll tales.

Work Cited

Stotsky, Sandra. "Research on Reading/Writing Relationships: A Synthesis and Suggested Directions," *Language Arts* 60 (May 1983): 627–42.

Suggested Reading List

Asbjornsen, Peter C., and Jorgen E. Moe. *East O' the Sun and West O' the Moon.* Macmillan, 1953.

Baker, Augusta, ed. *The Golden Lynx and Other Tales.* J. B. Lippincott, 1960. (See "Kari Woodencoat," 19–33)

Berenstain, Michael. *The Troll Book.* Random House, 1980.

Brown, Marcia. *The Three Billy Goats Gruff.* Harcourt Brace Jovanovich, 1972.

d'Aulaire, Ingri, and Edgar P. d'Aulaire. *Trolls.* Doubleday, 1972.

de Paola, Tomie. *Helga's Dowry: A Troll Love Story.* Harcourt Brace Jovanovich, 1977.

Fillmore, Parker. *Shepherd's Nosegay: Stories from Finland and Czechoslovakia.* Harcourt, Brace and World, 1958. (See "The Terrible Olli," 53–63)

Galdone, Paul. *The Three Billy Goats Gruff.* Houghton Mifflin, 1981.

Hatch, Mary C., ed. *More Danish Tales*. Harcourt, Brace and World, 1949. (See "The Seven Stars," 79–87; "The Princess with the Golden Shoes," 88–104; "The Boy Who Was Never Afraid," 182–98; and "The Golden Bird," 214–37)

Haviland, Virginia, ed. *Favorite Fairy Tales Told in Norway*. Little, Brown, 1961. (See "Boots and the Troll," 75–88)

Jones, Olive, and John Bauer. *In the Troll Wood*. Methuen, 1978.

Krensky, Stephen. *A Troll in Passing*. Atheneum, 1980.

Lobel, Anita. *The Troll Music*. Harper and Row, 1966.

McGovern, Ann. *Half a Kingdom: An Icelandic Folktale*. Warner, 1977.

Manning-Sanders, Ruth. *A Book of Ogres and Trolls*. Dutton, 1972. (See "Tritil, Litil and the Birds," 20–31; "John and the Troll Wife," 91–100; "The Troll's Little Daughter," 110–22; "Nils in the Forest," 123–27; "The Gold Knob," 38–43; and "Sigurd the King's Son," 53–65)

Marshall, Edward. *Troll Country*. Dial, 1980. (A beginning reader)

Minard, Rosemary. *Womenfolk and Fairy Tales*. Houghton Mifflin, 1975.

Olenius, Elsa, ed. *Great Swedish Fairy Tales*. Delacorte, 1973.

Stobbs, William. *The Three Billy Goats Gruff*. McGraw-Hill, 1968.

Torgersen, Don A. *The Girl Who Tricked the Troll*. Children's Press, 1978.

Joy F. Moss, University of Rochester, New York

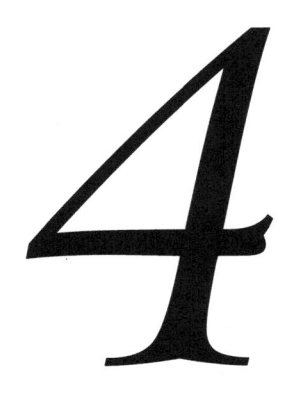

4 | EMPHASIS: INTEGRATING READING AND LITERATURE ACROSS THE CURRICULUM

PASTA POTPOURRI

WHO
Primary students; with adaptation, older students

WHY
This strategy orchestrates a variety of experiences across traditional subject matter areas by integrating the book *Strega Nona* by Tomie de Paola into the curriculum. It provides a multitude of activities in language arts and other subjects, using the book in many different ways over a period of time. The continual repetition and focus on the semantic, syntactic, and graphophonic systems as well as the illustrations provide the teacher with the necessary options for choosing those strategies and concepts that best meet the individual needs of the students.

HOW
Cooking
1. If cooking facilities are available, have students follow a recipe to make their own pasta. Cook the pasta and serve with butter and cheese.
2. Students follow a recipe to make alphabet soup with purchased alphabet pasta.

Math and Science
1. Students are given differing amounts of pasta shapes to make manipulative graphs, pictorial graphs, or abstract graphs.
2. The class works together to gather information on a topic and prepares a graph using pasta to present the findings.
3. The children string colored pasta according to a set pattern (such as red/red/blue, red/red/blue, red/red/blue).
4. Explain the concept of change by boiling pasta. Have students record their observations of the changes as the pasta progresses from rigid to bendable to soft to mushy.

5. As water boils, discuss the cycle of boiling water to steam to water vapor to condensation.

Fine Arts

1. Students use different types of pasta to create pasta collages or pasta people, and then write about their creations.
2. Students listen to "Capriccio Italian" by Peter Ilyich Tchaikovsky and discuss Tchaikovsky's perception of Italy.
3. Small or large groups of children can act out the following verse. Their movements reinforce the science concepts of cooking pasta.

> *Pasta Play*
> Be uncooked pasta.
> Throw yourself in the pot.
> Start to cook.
> Start to boil.
> Pour yourself on the plate.
> Toss yourself with the cheese.
> Wrap yourself around the fork.
> Get chewed up.
> Be swallowed!

Social Studies

1. Discuss and compare the concept of the witch, including cultural differences in the labels, expectations, and functions of witches.
2. Have students create imaginary potions for different occasions and write about their effects.
3. Discuss folk remedies of different cultures.

Language Arts

1. Children use different types of pasta to write their names or messages.
2. Use the chant below and have children clap, snap, and slap to the pattern of the chant. Use a chart to emphasize, delete, or exchange specific words to change the rhythm or the meanings.

> Bubble, bubble, pasta pot.
> Boil some pasta nice and hot.
> I'm hungry and it's time to sup.
> Boil enough pasta to fill me up.

Robert C. Wortman and Jackie Wortman, Tucson Unified School District, Arizona

ROBOT WALK

Children learn best about space, time, numbers, and language if they can "experience" them in some way. For that hands-on experience, use the Robot Walk in kindergarten and primary classes to:

Introduce the language of math (more than, less than, equal to)
Use precise language (left rather than over there)
Practice spatial concepts (left, right and up, down)

In this activity, students give directions to the robots, compare distances traveled, read a map, and extend the robot theme by writing a story and drawing illustrations.

Before class, draw a simple grid on the chalkboard like the one below. Label some points on the grid with familiar places in your neighborhood or town. Mark the locations of three robots. (If you have magnetic letters for your board, you can easily move them when students are giving directions to the robots.)

Begin by asking students to share their ideas of what a robot is. Have they ever seen a real robot? A make-believe robot on television or in the movies? What about C3PO and R2D2 from the soon-to-be-rereleased "Star Wars" films? Students can use their own language to talk about what robots look like and what they can do.

Now move on to the grid and ask students to direct these imaginary robots. They choose one destination for all three robots—a school, park, store, or any other landmark on the grid. Each robot must then take the shortest route to the destination. Students tell the robot to walk one block right, two blocks up, and so on. Try several routes for each robot, counting blocks to find the shortest route.

When all the robots have "walked" to the destination, compare the distances. Which robot walked the longest distance? The shortest? How many more blocks did the first robot walk than the second or third? Have students talk about how they figured out the answers.

There are many possibilities for extending the robot theme; most will be suggested by the students themselves. One idea is to have students write about the robots' walk. What happened when one robot was walking or after it arrived at the destination? What was the robot "thinking"? Encourage students to draw or describe what their story-robots look like.

(The idea for the Robot Walk comes from Comprehensive School Mathematics Program, CEMREL, Inc., © 1976. Used by permission of CSMP Mathematics for Kindergarten, Midcontinent Regional Educational Laboratory.)

Shirley R. Crenshaw with Constance Guy, Robert E. Lee School, Columbia, Missouri

BUBBLES THROUGHOUT
A Week-Long Integrated Learning Experience

WHY

Bubbles are a part of science and mathematics; they encourage curiosity and invite investigation and discovery. Curiosity encourages questioning and answering and lots of discussion. Bubbles can flow through all areas of the curriculum.

WHO

Students in kindergarten and grade 1

HOW

Day One
Assemble dishwashing soap, cups, straws, buckets, pouring and measuring equipment, a water table (if possible), egg beaters, towels, and a mop.

Present *Bubble, Bubble,* a wordless picture book by Mercer Mayer, by first just showing each illustration to the children. Then "read" the book, with children supplying the story text.

Lead a few children to the water table, where there is a bucket of soapy water and various water play equipment. Scoop about a half inch of water into a cup for each child; give each child a straw; and remind the children to blow out the soapy water, not to suck it through the straw. There will be a profusion of bubbles in the air and many comments, which are recorded on chart paper as the children talk ("Rainbows," says one child; "Look, ice cream," says another). At circle time talk about the experience and read aloud what the children said about their bubbles as they worked at the water table.

Day Two
Assemble 2" circles cut from construction paper, sheets of 8 1/2" x 11" paper, butcher paper, glue or rubber cement, crayons, a record player or tape deck, and records or tapes of "bubbly" music.

Start by reading *Leo the Late Bloomer Takes a Bath* by Robert Kraus et al. After talking about Leo's bathing experience, suggest that it might have helped if Leo could have turned the bubbles into something else. Hold up a circle, blow on it, and let it float to the floor. Then ask, "What else could this bubble be?" Encourage the youngsters to pretend that bubbles can become something else and to glue the bubbles (the circles) on paper to form other objects, adding details with crayons.

Prepare a cover page with one circle and the words "Once this was a bubble. . . ." As children finish their pictures, take their dictation, leading them into a language pattern by asking, "What is it now?" Students respond, "Now it's a nose," "Now it's a traffic light," "Now it's a Ford 4 x 4," or some other object containing one or more circles.

Assemble the picture and text pages together in an accordion book, made by taking a length of butcher paper, folding it in half lengthwise (for strength), and then folding the paper accordion style. Glue the children's pages to the folded butcher paper. At circle time each child can read his or her own page. Later this durable book may be displayed so that several children may read it at one time.

When the book is completed, students dance to the "bubbly" music. You may want to suggest some body movements, such as "Make your body into a bubble and roll around"; "Blow up bigger, bigger, bigger"; "Float away . . . Pop!"

Day Three
Assemble 1 1/2-inch circles in any two colors, 6-inch green circles, paper fish about 4 inches long, dots made by a hole puncher, paper bathtubs about 6 inches long, a large bathtub cut from butcher paper, glue or rubber cement, and marbles.

At circle time make a people graph by asking, "Who takes a bubble bath? Who does not?" Children line up on the floor according to their answers. Discuss which line is longer, and count the children in each line. Give each child a small circle of any color, representing a bubble. Each child writes his or her name on the circle and tapes or pins it on the large paper bathtub. The tub is divided in half, with one end labeled "I take bubble baths" and the other end labeled "I do not take bubble baths." Children discuss the concepts of more and less and count the bubbles on each side of the tub.

Children move to number stations where a particular number concept is highlighted; for example, six. At one table children may place six bubbles (small circles) on a small paper bathtub. They dictate how many of each color they've used: "Four pink and two blue, six bubbles in my tub." Children may make several tubs, varying the number of each of the two colored circles but always using six circles. At another table, children glue a fish onto a 6-inch circle (a fish bowl?) and glue six paper-punch dots near the fish's mouth, dictating something like, "One fish blows six bubbles." As time allows, work on invariance of number concepts with individual children by hiding and counting marbles.

Day Four

Assemble small balloons, vinegar, baking soda, a clear plastic bottle (such as the one the vinegar comes in), paper, crayons, lemonade and limeade, cups, spoons.

At circle time reread the accordion bubble book. Then students form small groups and discuss what is a solid, a liquid, and a gas. Perform the following experiment for each group. Pour a half inch of vinegar into the plastic bottle. Place a heaping teaspoon of baking soda into the bottle and immediately put the mouth of a balloon over the top of the bottle. The balloon inflates. When it is fully inflated, carefully pull the balloon off and knot it.

Later, mix the lemonade and limeade for snack time and give each child a cup of juice. Carry around a bowl containing the baking soda and let each child place a teaspoonful of the baking soda into his or her cup, instantly producing lemon-lime soda. Ask the children to draw something about the experience and to write (or dictate) what they are drawing. Write the soda recipe on chart paper.

Day Five

Assemble a copy of *Billy Balloon*, salt, flour, blue coloring, water, oil, a toaster oven (if possible), aluminum foil, soap, cups, and straws.

Read *Billy Balloon* aloud and encourage the children to read along during a second reading. Talk about how balloons are like bubbles. Ask them to look around the room for things that begin with the letter B.

Make a batch of blue clay (another B word) with the salt, flour, blue coloring, and oil, or bring in blue Play-Doh. Encourage students to make B objects, such as birds, boats, bananas, and butterflies. Let each child make one item to keep. Place these on foil and bake them in the oven.

Wind up the activity by getting out soapy water, cups, and straws and by going outside to blow bubbles. Encourage children to talk and think about the other bubble activities and to review their completed bubble projects.

Wendy Hood, Hollinger Elementary School, Tucson, Arizona

LEARNING AND WRITING ABOUT MAGNETS

Nothing gets young students hooked on science quicker than magnets. They are fascinated by the seemingly magical qualities of magnets, and their excitement helps them to write about their experiences.

Exploring science requires students to use language as they ask questions and write down their observations. I have my students record their impressions about the magnet experiments they perform or observe. In doing so, they develop their writing skills, as well as learn new science words and the importance of using exact language in observation.

Introduce students to the activity by setting out several magnets, a collection of small objects made of a variety of metals and other materials, several sheets of cardboard, and a box of paper clips. Let the students investigate the magnets without directions. Ask only that they write down what they find out about the magnets. Encourage students to use drawings to show what they mean.

The students read their writings to the entire class to initiate discussion of the properties of magnets. I'm always impressed with the information students discover on their own.

Have several specific tasks organized in boxes or dishpans, each with a statement of instruction. After students explore and write on their own and discuss their writings, designate pairs of students, or groups of three or four, and let each group choose a task. Try to have enough supplies so that several groups can perform the same experiment simultaneously. Let students know that they will all have a chance to perform each task.

A set of tasks for magnets might include the following:

Task 1:   Find out what kinds of things the magnet will pick up. Sort each object into the "yes" or "no" pan and record the items that the magnet attracted.
Materials: a variety of odds and ends (candle, penny, nail, spool, jar lid, pencil, foil, etc.), a pan labeled "yes" and a pan labeled "no," a magnet

Task 2:   Test each magnet's strength by holding a piece of cardboard between it and a paper clip. Try different magnets, and try placing two pieces of cardboard between the magnet and the paper clip. What happens?
Materials: paper clips, at least two magnets of different strengths, several pieces of cardboard

Task 3:   Attach a paper clip to the magnet. What happens? Try attaching a second paper clip to the first. Try adding other paper clips to form a chain. What happens?
Materials: paper clips, magnet

Task 4:   Try touching two ends marked *N* and *S* together. Touch *S* to *S; N* to *N*. What happens? Why?
Materials: two bar magnets labeled *N* and *S*

As a final activity, ask students to write down their thoughts on what they found out about magnets and to illustrate the pages. Bind all the pages together and put the book in the science area for all to read.

I do not grade or correct the students' pages, other than noting what the student reads to me if I can't decipher it on my own. Technical writing skills can be acquired at a later time. At this point, the value for the students is in the process of doing the task, thinking about the problem, and using symbols and words that they know to record what they observed.

Sharron Cadieux, Mill Glen Road School, Winchendon, Massachusetts

HATCHING EGGS AND IDEAS

WHY

- To use repetitious language and illustrations to enhance students' comprehension
- To encourage students to make predictions as they read
- To reduce students' apprehensions about reading by having them read a story in a group

WHO

Reluctant readers, beginning readers who are having difficulty with reading and writing, or readers who are just beginning to integrate reading with writing

HOW

Write the title of the book *The Happy Egg* by Ruth Krauss on the board and read it aloud with the class. Show the book cover to the group and ask if anyone has heard the story. Ask what students believe the book will be about. Read the story as far as "So it got sat on and sat on and sat on and sat on. . . ." Pause and ask students to predict the text on the following page. Continue to read the story, pausing periodically to ask children to fill in a missing word or to predict the next illustration and its text.

Reread the story with the children joining in. Ask them to retell the story. Then discuss what the children already know about hatching eggs. Encourage them to think of clues in the story that indicate how long it takes to hatch eggs, and to remember what the illustrations show. Discuss what birds can do that eggs cannot.

Children may use flannel-board pictures to retell the story to one another. Working individually or in groups, they may write or dictate stories using the same format as *The Happy Egg* to show the development of other creatures, real or imaginary. Encourage children to make and use puppets to act out *The Happy Egg* or their own stories, or interest them in preparing and presenting a dramatized version of *The Happy Egg* to another class. Children might use toy birds encased in Play-Doh or L'Eggs hosiery containers as they retell the story.

WHAT ELSE

1. Use the factual stories written by the children as additional reading for a science unit.
2. Plan a hunt for real eggs as a field trip. In advance, discuss where various nests are located and why they are not to be disturbed. Ask students to make notes or drawings of their discoveries.
3. When an active nest is visible from the classroom, *The Happy Egg* may spark discussion of comparisons and contrasts to the real nest.
4. Obtain a fertile egg of a reptile or amphibian. Contrast its development with the egg in *The Happy Egg*.
5. Collect various eggs or pictures of eggs and discuss their varying color, size, and texture.
6. Crack open an infertile egg and a fertile egg from hens and ask students to compare the two. Explain that eggs purchased at the store are infertile.
7. Locate factual information about eggs hatching. Ask the children to compare the two types of writing.
8. Plant beans; when they sprout, start incubating eggs and plant additional beans. Students can measure the bean plants on a regular basis and can compare and contrast the development of the animals and the plants.
9. Students prepare illustrations showing the passage of time.
10. Read aloud *Chickens Aren't the Only Ones* by Ruth Heller.

Mary R. Watson, Community Education Center, Columbia, Missouri

| WRITING AS SCIENTISTS

PURPOSE

- To use writing to make predictions and observations about science experiments

MATERIALS

- Paper, pencils
- Materials necessary to perform simple science experiments

While planning a science unit that included several simple experiments, I looked for a way to integrate reading and writing into the unit. When one of my kindergartners, excited about the experiments we were going to perform, asked me if he could write about them in his journal, it occurred to me that this would be a good opportunity for students to use writing to record predictions and observations.

The three experiments involved were placing a stalk of celery in a glass full of colored water, growing crystals from salt or sugar, and sprouting seeds in a clear jar. Before we began the first experiment, I explained to my students that science experiments are often performed in a laboratory, called a lab for short, where special equipment is available to the scientist. I told students that like scientists working in a lab, we would be writing "lab reports" about our experiments.

I pointed out that a scientist doesn't always find the information that he or she is looking for; sometimes an experiment turns out very differently than he or she expected. The lab report contains details about the experiment that can help the scientist understand the results of the experiment, and it can be an important reference if the experiment is repeated.

As a group, we brainstormed a list of information that should be included in each lab report. This list included the materials needed to complete the experiment, the steps involved, and observations on the results of the experiment. Then we performed the first experiment, and I distributed paper and pencils for students to use in writing their first lab reports.

The second and third experiments that we performed each had a "wait time" (the time between the onset of the experiment and when results could be observed). During this time I asked students to write predictions of what they thought would happen. Students finished writing their lab reports when the experiment was completed. By the time we had performed the third experiment, students were at home in their roles as amateur scientists and were able to record the steps, make predictions, and take notes on the results without consulting me.

Judi La Due, Iliff Preschool Kindergarten, Denver, Colorado

COMPETENT COMMUNICATORS

Who wouldn't rather hear a *story* than a *lecture?* Whether your class is studying the birds, the bees, or the wildebeests, a guest speaker with personal anecdotes and photographs will stimulate student interest more than any amount of lecturing or research. An activity centering around a guest speaker makes students more competent communicators by getting them involved in:

- Critical reading to prepare questions and phrase answers
- Careful listening to record information
- Speaking and writing to share with others the facts that impressed them

Our first-grade class was fortunate enough to find a doctoral student who raises cockatiels.

To find your own guest speaker, try asking your colleagues for ideas, asking your students for suggestions, asking students if their parents have personal knowledge of the topic, and writing to local townspeople or college students who have an interest in the topic. Once you've made the initial contact with the chosen speaker, let your students show their interest by drafting a class invitation. As the scribe for the class, you write the letter on the board as it is dictated and ask students to read it back carefully to make sure that no vital information has been left out. Do students say where and when they would like the visitor to arrive? Is a room number given? Write a final copy of the letter and encourage students to draw pictures to accompany the letter and to write individual messages on their pictures. Include these personal invitations with the group invitation when you mail it to the guest speaker.

Allow students several class periods to read books and magazines about the topic, in preparation for phrasing questions that are detailed and specific. After these reading sessions, you can inspire question writing by starting a list of *Facts Known* on the board. Supply a category such as *What birds look like* and ask students to call out their ideas. The completed list reminds students what they already know about birds, and can be left on the board to be updated after the speaker visits. My students developed the following list:

What birds look like
  feathers
  different colors
  different beaks
  wings
  different feet
  different sizes

Where birds live
  nests
  bird houses
  cages in a house

What birds do
  fly
  hop
  make nests
  find food
  feed babies
  lay eggs
  take baths
  sing
  some talk

What birds eat
  worms
  berries
  seeds
  bread
  crumbs
  water

After students devise questions to ask the guest speaker, they can read their questions aloud to one another and talk about how they would answer each question, based on what they already know. To ensure that each student has the chance to ask at least one question, have students select one or two questions each, the ones that they most want the speaker to answer. Write these questions on chart paper, including the student's name, so that students can read their own questions aloud on the day the guest speaker visits. At that time, students take turns asking questions and the speaker answers by giving facts, showing photos, and sharing memories of incidents that illustrate the point. (Our speaker brought photos not only of her birds but of the eggs from which they hatched.) Students who are not asking questions can keep notepads handy and jot down details to be added to the fact list. My students made these notes:

> Cockatiels can talk and learn words.
> Cockatiels feet have 3 toes in the front and 1 in the back.
> Cockatiels are covered with different colored feathers.

The notes that students take help them to update their *Facts Known* list. Even as the activity concluded, with a discussion of the updated fact list, the enthusiasm and accomplishment felt by my students ran high. After attentive reading, questioning, listening, and sharing of new ideas, they saw themselves, and rightly so, as *competent communicators.*

Carol Hittleman. Dix Hills, New York

ALL THE THINGS
WE CAN DO

WHY

To heighten students' awareness of themselves as learners by incorporating and integrating cognitive, affective, and motor learning across the curriculum

WHO

Kindergartners

HOW

To begin this unit, assemble the class outside or in the gym and talk about all the different ways we can move: running, crawling, sliding, hopping, and so forth. Encourage children to think about which parts of their bodies they use as they explore the different ways they can move. Set up painting, drawing, and writing areas nearby and encourage the children to write about and illustrate what they are doing. These might form part of a classroom display of "Things We Can Do."

If possible, take photos of the children as they move in different ways, and display the photos with the children's added captions. Later, collate the photos and captions into a book for the reading area. These books might be used for science activities by comparing how animals and humans move.

Music

Start this session with a discussion about the ways we can use specific body parts, such as "We clap our hands," "We stamp our feet." Teach one of the favorite movement songs, such as "What Can You Do, Punchinello, Funny Fellow?" and invite the children to tell, in turn, what body part they are going to move. The other children join in by imitating the action.

For another version of the game, write the children's suggested actions on chart paper; then invite them to select an action to act out. Ask children to read aloud each written choice or to tell how they knew which action they were choosing. This gives insight into their knowledge about print.

Select another action song, such as "Clap, Clap, Clap Your Hands." Teach the song first; then write the words on a poster, discussing the words with the children as you write. With those words that are likely to have personal relevance for the children, you might say something like, "How do I start writing *clap*? It starts the same way as your name, Claire. What do you think comes next?" When you have finished writing, children may notice and talk about the repetition of many words. They may want to point to some of the words and phrases as they sing the song. Ask children what else they could do besides clap. Their action words can be written on small cards, and the children can take turns putting the new words over the word clap. Then they can sing and dramatize their new versions.

Leave the poster and sets of alternative action words where the children can explore them independently and use them as a print resource for personal writing. Many other popular children's songs, rhymes, and finger plays lend themselves to this kind of treatment.

Physical Education

A well-planned outdoor area or physical education lesson provides another rich source of language. Set up a variety of equipment for the children to move over, under, in, out, through, along, and so on, and encourage them to verbalize what they are doing. Photos taken during this time can stimulate further discussion and can be added to the classroom display of "Things We Can Do."

Carpentry

Set up a woodwork area with such materials as nails of different lengths, polystyrene, wood, plastic bottle tops for wheels, margarine lids, and fabric scraps. Store the equipment in labeled containers. Have writing and drawing materials nearby for those who might like to draw plans, make lists, or record in writing what they have done. A simple plan for making an object could be introduced, and perhaps a parent could demonstrate how to build and use the object. If children show interest, a few very simple plans covered with clear adhesive-backed paper could be included in the area. Photos could be taken of the finished objects and made into a class book.

Cooking

Cooking can be a wonderful literacy experience. Prior to undertaking actual cooking, the children can practice pouring, measuring, beating, stirring, and mixing water and sand. At snack time they can help with the cutting, peeling, shredding, and serving of fruit and vegetables. This will give them experience with the concepts and the language that they will encounter in cooking. Explore samples of environmental print such as the containers for sugar, flour, and margarine, which the children are likely to encounter in cooking.

Introduce the cooking activity with a story such as *The Little Red Hen, The Gingerbread Man,* or *The Little Old Man Who Could Not Read.* You might improvise on *The Little Red Hen* so that she grew corn instead of wheat and wanted to make popcorn instead of bread. Explain how we find out how to cook something. Show the children a recipe book and how to use the index to locate a desired recipe. Read a simple recipe aloud to the children. Ask them to look for sample wrappers and containers of the ingredients in the class environmental print collection. Now write the recipe onto a poster, adding samples of environmental print alongside the words to serve as clues to their meaning.

Assemble the necessary ingredients and cooking utensils. Include a few items that you don't need. Now look at the recipe with the children and ask them to select only the necessary ingredients by matching the ingredients with the words on the recipe. Be sure to ask the children to tell you how they are making their decisions.

Follow the instructions on the recipe, taking photos to record the various steps. Display the photos as a story on the wall, and later collate them into a book for shared reading. Be sure to get a photo of the children enjoying the results of their cooking. Encourage them to write their own stories about the activity or to record the event with their own illustration.

"We Can Write Lots of Things"

Spend some time looking at the wall displays together and encourage the children to recall all the "Things We Can Do." Suggest that they share their accomplishments by inviting their families and friends to visit the classroom. Ask the children to decide on the necessary information to include and the wording for an invitation to visit the classroom and see their work. Make copies for the children to take home, and place an invitation on the bulletin board. Leave a notepad and pencil by the bulletin board and set out a box for the responses from home. Each day the children can collect and read the mail. At the appointed time, the children can act as hosts and share a sample of their cooking and a copy of the recipe with the visitors.

Provide the children with folders and invite them to select the writings that they want to keep. Date the writings to record each child's development, and set a time for a weekly conference with each child about the selections, discussing the changes taking place in both the function and form of that child's writing. This folder can go home at the end of the year as a present to the parents, a lovely memento of a period in their child's development.

Brenda Parkes, Brisbane College of Advanced Education, Mt. Gravatt, Queensland, Australia

| READ IT WITH MUSIC

WHY

Songs are a natural for classroom language development: they are enjoyable and require no explanation or motivation. The rhyme, rhythm, and repetition of verse and chorus heighten the predictability of the language. Reading songs becomes highly successful because students have the opportunity to read and reread predictable and familiar language. Song reading is a natural way to introduce print without any picture cues.

It is important to remember that songs will aid reading growth even if they are not read, since they expand the language base of the reader. However, there are many ways to use songs with print in order to take advantage of an enjoyable activity and make it a literacy experience.

WHO

All elementary students

HOW

Various activities that integrate music, reading, and writing are described below. The following guidelines will enhance each activity:

1. Songs invite repetition. Use them again and again. With younger children, repeat them daily.
2. Introduce songs by singing them. Let the children read along as they are learning the words, but don't make the reading a chore. It's easier for them to read a song after they have learned it.
3. Always focus on the whole when using song sheets or posters. Point to entire sentences during a sing-along, not at each word.

Shared Songs

Write the words to a simple, repetitive song on the board. Sing the song with the group several times, focusing on the written words as you sing, until the children are familiar with the song. Continue to sing the song each day, allowing students to take turns being song leader and guiding the singing. Copy the song onto chart paper or poster board so that it can be used over and over. The pages might be illustrated and bound into a Big Book for the classroom. Some appropriate songs to use are "I Love the Mountains," "Hush Little Baby," and "If You're Happy and You Know It."

Individual Student Books

As a perfect follow-up (suggested by author Bill Martin, Jr., in a workshop at Oakland University) to the shared books, prepare small books for students to read at the reading table or reading corner. Using half sheets of typing paper, type or write one line of the song on each page and staple the pages inside a cover made from cutting a file folder in half. For longer songs, put one verse on each page. Decorate and laminate the cover. The pages may be illustrated or left plain, providing a pictureless reading experience. Older students can prepare their own books.

Singing Signboards

Signboards can be made for any repetitive song, such as "She'll Be Comin' 'Round the Mountain," "I Love My Rooster," "There Was an Old Woman

Who Swallowed a Fly," and "If You're Happy and You Know It." Write each repetitive phrase or verse on small strips of tagboard and the chorus on larger sheets of tagboard or on poster board. Use the signboards in these activities:

1. Hold all the cards (or ask a student to) and turn them over as the song is sung, or place them on a chart board, allowing children to read the words as they sing. Later make this a sort of guessing-song game, silently holding up the next verse to be sung.
2. Ask students to hold up signboards as the class sings a song. Each student holds his or her card down until the class sings the verse on the sign. This activity is a natural to share with another class once students have rehearsed it several times.
3. Establish a place where students can use the signboards with another student or as an independent activity. Children can repeat the class activities or invent their own.

Using the Listening Post or Tape Center

When students know a song well, the words can be tape-recorded for the class listening post. Students use the tape as a read-along with books made in the classroom or trade books. To make the tape, assemble a book, a tape recorder, a blank tape (preferably a ten-or twenty-minute cassette so both sides can be used with a minimum of rewinding), and a clicker, a pair of rhythm sticks, or another noisemaker. After students rehearse singing the song with one student using the clicker to indicate when to turn the page, tape-record the song. This is a perfect time to talk about record and tape production. The classroom becomes a recording studio, and several "takes" might be needed before the recording is acceptable. Older students might work individually or in groups to tape-record a book for younger students.

Writing Song Books

Many songs suggest original verses. Some, such as "Put Your Finger in the Air," are very simple and work well with younger students. Others, such as "Hey Lolly," are more complex. Other songs can also be rewritten and personalized. Use these invented songs to make illustrated class books, with a verse on each page. These songs can also be tape-recorded for the listening post.

Song Sheets

Older students will enjoy classroom song sheets. Start with one page and add on as the year continues. Several songs can appear on each page, perhaps grouped by theme. Song sheets are versatile—they can be used daily in a self-contained class, and they are also wonderful for a substitute teacher. Don't worry if young children don't really read the words at first. They will be reading the lyrics before long.

Extending Song Sheets

1. Many records come with printed song sheets. Make a tape recording of the song and add it and the song sheet to the listening center. Ella Jenkins, a children's folksinger, is ideal for listening-post singalongs. Tapes and song sheets of some popular music might also be added to the listening center.
2. Invite children to prepare song sheets for some favorite works of popular music. This is a complex literacy task that children will enjoy.
3. Invite children to construct scrapbooks to serve as class songbooks. The songbooks can be a year-long project used for sing-alongs, or they can serve as an end-of-the-year collection of old favorites of the children.

Song Bees

Song bees are an old camp game. Divide the class into teams and select a word. In turn, each team sings a song that contains the word. A team is eliminated if the students cannot think of an appropriate song, and the game continues until only one team remains, as in a spelling bee. Thematic words work best, or give students a general concept, such as water, and let them use variations of the concept, such as rain, snow, ocean, sea, drinking, crying, tears.

Expand the song bee into a literacy experience by giving the teams time to list their songs in advance of the bee. Or announce a theme at the beginning of the week to give teams time to look for songs. On the day of the bee, teams sing the songs they have found.

Debra Goodman, Detroit Public Schools, Michigan

I CAN READ
NURSERY RHYMES

WHY

To integrate language and art activities through the use of the highly predictable, rhyming, and rhythmic language patterns of nursery rhymes

WHO

Kindergartners

HOW

Assemble the following materials: a collection of nursery rhymes, chart paper containing outlines of nursery rhyme characters and appropriate backgrounds, blank chart paper, felt-tip pens, and such collage materials as tissue paper, crepe paper, vinyl and fabric scraps, buttons, margarine and fruit juice lids, used wrapping paper, ribbons, wood shavings, pasta dyed in a range of colors, dyed Popsicle sticks, yarn, leaves, bark, and sticks. It is important to use a wide variety of materials to invite sensory and language learning. Your own local area will yield many other examples.

Introduce a nursery rhyme orally; have the children repeat it aloud with you. When they are comfortable with the rhyme, improvise on how you say it:

- You say one line, children say the next
- Boys say one character's part, girls say the other
- You act as narrator, children take the character parts
- Clap the rhythm of the rhyme as all say it aloud
- Clap the rhythm without saying the words
- Accompany the words with percussion instruments

Write the rhyme on chart paper to help everyone remember it. Be sure to elicit the children's help with decisions about writing the rhyme—what to write first so that everyone knows the name of the rhyme, where to write next, what letters might be used in some of the words, and so on. In this way you are demonstrating to students a purposeful function of writing, an ongoing dialogue using metalinguistic terms in the context of their use, and a model of the writing process. As you create this classroom resource together, you are also giving the class a degree of ownership of the words as children help to create the experience chart.

Have the children work in small groups to create a collage to accompany the rhyme. As they work, encourage them to discuss the characters, what they say and do, and how they look. Display the pictures with the words and have the students say the rhyme aloud once again. You may wish to return to the earlier improvisations, this time using the print to identify the parts. For this reason, you might want to use different colors to signify verse and chorus or the words of different characters.

As each nursery rhyme is introduced, add the text and accompanying collages to your display until you have a nursery rhyme collage mural. This will be a valuable resource for children in activities involving word phrases and title matching, in choosing their parts in shared readings, for musical accompaniment, and as a general print resource for children's reading and writing.

WHAT ELSE

Provide the children with the words and illustrations for several different nursery rhymes. Have them decide which words go with each illustration, thus giving insights into their present strategies for dealing with print. Copies of the pairs of nursery rhyme text and illustrations could be glued to sheets of paper and collated into personal books for the children to take home to share with their families. In printing the words, be sure to leave room for children to add their own writing. Alternatively, provide the illustrations only and invite children to write their own versions of the nursery rhymes.

Brenda Parkes, Brisbane College of Advanced Education, Mt. Gravatt, Queensland, Australia

KALEIDOSCOPE DESIGNS

To create kaleidoscope designs, students tear tissue paper of different colors into small pieces and arrange the pieces on sheets of waxed paper, one sheet of waxed paper per student. The torn pieces of tissue paper should overlap slightly, filling a circular area approximately six inches in diameter. A second sheet of waxed paper is placed over the circular area and pressed with a warm iron, causing the two sheets of waxed paper to adhere and "trap" the tissue paper design. (You might place a sheet of newspaper on top of the waxed paper to prevent wax buildup on the iron.) When the paper cools, students place a circular shape over the design and trace around the edge. (A Frisbee works well.) Each circular design is then cut out, and two slightly larger circles of construction paper, one inch in width, are glued together with the design in between, creating a frame.

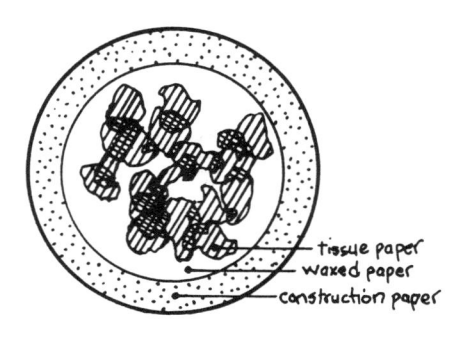

As part of this activity, I discussed primary and secondary colors with my students and introduced design elements such as balance and line, using finished designs as examples. I also discovered that the designs could be projected on a screen using an overhead projector. Students viewed classmates' designs, brainstormed for descriptive words and phrases, and talked about what the images made them think of. The brightly colored abstract shapes and colors inspired poems of varying moods, which, along with the designs, were shared with students from another class in a slightly darkened room to a background of soft music.

Nancy Riley, Greenwood Forest Elementary School, Houston, Texas

A CLASSROOM TIME MACHINE

PURPOSE

- To learn about past peoples and cultures and about important historical events

MATERIALS

- A very large cardboard box
- A clothes pole or dowel, a sheet, a brad
- Tempera paints, a paintbrush
- A cassette tape recorder with headphones
- Several cassette tapes

A classroom time machine is my way of making the events studied in social studies and history especially real to students. With the help of everyone's imagination and a few props, students can travel beyond the walls of the classroom and experience historical events as if they were present.

A time machine can be built fairly simply from a large cardboard wardrobe box (or from two refrigerator boxes put together). I cut out the top and one side of the box and attach a clothes pole at the top of the open side. A bed sheet attached to this pole provides a curtained entrance. I then paint the box to resemble a spaceship. Using a brad to attach a thin, short strip of cardboard to the outside of the box, I create a gauge. In one position, the lever points to the words "Preparing for Takeoff"; in the other position, the lever points to "Flight in Progress." Before entering the time machine, the student moves the lever to "Flight in Progress" so that he or she will not be interrupted.

To prepare a trip to a past event and place, I record a five-to ten-minute narrative. I coordinate my narrative with visual aids that I attach in numbered sequence inside the box. Appropriate visual aids might include such items as drawings, diagrams, maps, reproductions of paintings, study prints, and photos. Some libraries and museums lend pictures and artifacts for a minimal fee. I then place the cassette recorder, tape, and headphones on the floor inside the time machine, which is kept at the side or back of the room so that students can use it unobtrusively throughout the day.

A flight schedule of assigned times can be used to regulate the flow of students. When explaining the activity, I encourage students to help me think of rules for travel: "If the current time traveler is not done on time, wait at your desk for your turn"; "Remember to rewind the tape before leaving the time machine." I write these rules on a sheet of posterboard and attach it to the outside of the time machine. Making an extra copy or two of the current tape in case of accidental erasure is wise.

Time travel trips can be adapted to virtually any social studies or history topic, and the narrative approach can be varied from trip to trip. For instance, one narrative might take students on a sightseeing trip through ancient Egypt, pointing out features of interest and describing customs in the manner of a tour guide. Another narrative might begin by informing the student that he or she will experience one day in the life of a newcomer to Plymouth Rock in the year 1621, and then describe everything that the student sees and does in that one day. Yet another approach would be to invite a famous figure from the past to meet and share information with the student time traveler.

I provide follow-up worksheets to help students think about what they heard and saw on their trip, and hold a class discussion on each time travel presentation after all students have visited it. Students' maturity often determines their ability to work in groups to plan additional time travel trips, which requires assembling visual aids, writing scripts, and recording them on cassettes. The best time travel trips can be saved and used again year after year to spice up the study of social studies and history.

Penny Rawson, Oak Park, Illinois

AN ECONOMICS LESSON ON SCARCITY

WHY

Scarcity is a basic premise for understanding economic systems. The following activities are designed to follow a progression of understanding on the topics of scarcity, needs, wants, and decision making. Reading and writing will support economic learning.

WHO

Primary students; with adaptation, older students

HOW

Scarcity

Begin the lesson on scarcity by presenting to the class the following problem: "We have twelve apples and thirty students. Are there enough apples for everyone to have one?" Divide the class into four groups and give each group three apples. If available, have an aide or parent serve as group leader, or select a student leader for each group.

Ask each group to brainstorm ideas for solving the problem and to list the ideas on paper. Students are to analyze each solution, discussing whether it is fair or possible. Students in each group decide which solution they like best and select a reporter to announce this decision. The full class reassembles to hear and discuss each group's decision. Steer the discussion back to the original problem and explain that it has a name: scarcity. Then give every child an apple and ask if there is a scarcity now. Explain that when there is no scarcity, objects are found in abundance and are sometimes free.

Scarcity can also be demonstrated in a game that is the reverse of Musical Chairs. Begin with an equal number of chairs and children, perhaps six. When the music stops, each child sits in a chair. Explain that all the children have their needs satisfied. Then add one child and resume the game. When the music stops, one child cannot sit in a chair. Explain that this child's need is not satisfied. Ask children for possible solutions. They might suggest that two children share a chair. Play the game a few more times, each time adding one child. Ask students to observe whether their solutions will work and to identify what was scarce during the game.

Use Mother Goose rhymes and other favorite children's tales to reinforce the concept of scarcity. For example, "Old Mother Hubbard," "The Three Billy Goats Gruff," "The Lion, the Boar and the Vultures," "Jack and the Beanstalk," *The Bean Boy* by Joan Chase Bowden, and *Socks for Supper* by Jack Kent all present situations where there is a scarcity. Read aloud *Stone Soup* by Marcia Brown and ask children to bring in things to make stone soup in the classroom.

Needs

To introduce the concept of needs, bring to class a plant and an animal (such as a gerbil, rat, hamster, or fish). Explain that both the plant and animal require certain things to stay alive. These are called needs. Ask children to suggest what the plant will need and what the animal will need to stay alive. As children brainstorm, write their suggestions on the board. Invite students to compare the two lists of needs.

Next, children might brainstorm a list of their personal needs, such as food, shelter, clothing, and love. If students mention things that are not a necessity, explain that these items are called wants. Ask children to review and compare the lists of needs for the plant, the animal, and themselves.

Needs and Wants

To compare needs and wants, have students form small groups and ask them to brainstorm a list of all the things they want but don't need. Students discuss why they don't have all of these things, suggesting limited income, limited raw resources, limited time, and so on. Next, ask children to draw a picture of themselves and to make a collage of the things they want by cutting and pasting pictures from magazines and catalogs. Then they write about what they want and why.

Display the group lists and ask students to determine the ten most popular wants. List these items on a survey sheet and ask the children to select their own favorite item or perhaps two items. Pair children with partners and let them survey each other. Graph the results for all to see. Students might then survey other students in the same grade in the school. Graph these results and ask the class to compare the two graphs. You might break down the results by first and second choice or by sex, asking children to draw conclusions and inferences as to whether boys and girls have different wants.

Decision Making

Assemble colored squares of construction paper about one inch square and assign one color to different kinds of desserts (such as pie, cake, cookies, ice cream) or main dishes (pizza, hamburgers, tacos, hot dogs) or even vegetables (carrots, peas, broccoli, corn). Prepare a chart on the bulletin board listing the four food items.

Ask students to hypothesize which items will be the two most popular choices in the class. Then ask students to take turns making a selection by putting a paper marker on the board in the appropriate category. (Markers might be attached with push pins or tape.) Discuss the results and the accuracy of students' hypotheses.

Initiate another decision-making activity by reviewing the concept of a want and by explaining that students are to make a class collage of wants. Review the concept of scarcity, reminding students that they cannot have everything they want. Ask students to select from a catalog or magazine a picture of one item that they want. Students glue the pictures to butcher paper to make a class collage of wants. Students might also examine the choices that others make by asking a partner what item he or she selected and why. Students announce their partner's choice and the reason, such as "John wants a football because it is his favorite sport." Discuss how individuals have different wants because each person is unique.

WHAT ELSE

Read fairy tales or wishing stories to the class to illustrate the economic conflict between unlimited wants and limited resources. Some possible stories are Aesop, *The Goose That Laid the Golden Egg* and *The Grasshopper and the Ant;* Lorna Balian, *Sweet Touch;* Dick Gackenbach, *Hattie Rabbit;* Brothers Grimm, *The Fisherman and His Wife* and *The Golden Goose;* and Leo Lionni, *Alexander and the Wind-Up Mouse*

References

Gray, Polly. "Why Can't I Have It?" *The Elementary Economist 1*, no. 1. The National Center of Economic Education for Children, Lesley College.

Kniep, Willard M. *Economics Exchange: Teaching Economics in Elementary School,* 12–13. Kendall/Hunt, 1981.

Willard Kniep, Global Perspectives in Education, New York, New York, and Sandra Lee Smith, Phoenix Elementary School District #1, Arizona

WRITING POSTCARDS FROM SCRATCH

"Having a wonderful time. Wish you were here." You can't fit much more than that in the 2" x 3" writing area on a picture postcard. And while this restrictive format may not encourage elaborate expression, it suits its purpose: to help travelers remember those at home with minimum effort.

This activity introduces a new purpose for the picture postcard: through the use of postcards, photographs, and language, students become involved with another culture or geographical location. After talking about the types of cultural information presented in the photographs and in the printed captions describing the scenes on some sample picture postcards, students cull glossy photos from travel magazines and brochures, research facts to explain the scenes in the photographs, write captions for the photographs and messages to friends, and turn out their own "picture postcards" using rectangles of poster board. The completed postcards, though not appropriate for actual mailing, can be "sent" to other students in the class or school.

You will need to assemble the following materials:

- *National Geographic* magazines, travel magazines, and travel brochures from local travel agencies
- Sample informational/picture postcards from other countries
- 5" x 7" rectangles of white poster board
- Fine-point markers, rulers, scissors, glue

Begin by passing around the sample postcards. Have students look at the scenes and take turns reading aloud the printed captions on the reverse side. Ask them about the information they learn from the cards. Does the caption tell more about the scene? What kinds of details are given?

Have students leaf through the magazines and brochures and cut out photographs to feature on their picture postcards. Each photograph should depict either an aspect of life in another culture (a table spread with native delicacies, a holiday celebration); a landscape (the Sahara Desert, the Nile River); or a historical attraction (the Great Wall of China, the Eiffel Tower). And if any students care to, they may choose more than one photo depicting the same subject matter and snip out portions of each to assemble for a collage effect.

To write a descriptive caption for the photo (to go on the reverse side of the postcard), each student needs to research a few background facts. Remind students to check first the magazines from which they took the photos. The class can suggest other ways to find the necessary information, such as encyclopedias, atlases, special books on specific countries, and tourist guides.

A single class period spent in the library is probably enough to give students the facts they need to draft the captions. Make sure that they understand the limits of the postcard format; at most, two or three sentences describing the photograph will fit above or below the message on the postcard. As students write their descriptions, classmates can help them to decide what information to include. Advise students to show the photograph to someone else and ask, "Look at this picture and then tell me what you would most like to know about the person (or place or thing) shown here."

Finally, students glue the photographs or photo collages onto 5" x 7" rectangles of poster board. By drawing a line from top to bottom on the blank side of the card to divide it in half, students provide a space on the right for the address (fictional or real) and stamp (drawn on or cut out of colored paper and glued on), and a space on the left for the finished caption and a message. If you use this activity with upper elementary students, have them copy their captions onto the actual postcards; let younger students write the text on a separate page and have their captions reduced at a photocopying shop so that the captions can be glued on in the space allotted. (Or to save time, copy the captions onto the postcards yourself.)

At this point, students have their picture postcards in front of them, complete except for the greeting. To inspire original messages, ask each student to make his or her message an explanation of why he or she has decided during this "trip" never to return home. Or ask each student to imagine that he or she has visited the same site a hundred times, and to describe why he or she still finds the trip interesting. As students individualize their postcards with messages to real or imaginary friends, you can be sure that they'll employ more thought and imagination than was ever spent on "Having a wonderful time. Wish you were here."

Janis P. Hunter, Fort Loramie Elementary School, Fort Loramie, Ohio